Welcome To My World

Selected Poems

1973-2013

DAVID PRASHKER

THE ARGAMAN PRESS

The Argaman Press

ISBN: 0692207015
ISBN-13: 978-0692207017

7

David Prashker's "Selected Poems 1973-2013" are drawn from these privately printed collections:

Early Poems (1981)
Hebrew Poems (1984)
Khaki On Both Sides (1986)
Japanese Poems (1989)
Coins (1993)
The Pulse (1998)
The Strings on the Dome of the Tortoise (2003)
The Caged Songbird of the Muse (2008)
The Word and the Temple (2013)

CONTENTS

Welcome To My World

Welcome to my world,
    it's made of light seeping through darkness,
where failure is acknowledged, but with nothing to repent.
Where zero is both nothing
    and perfection of the starkness,
and destiny is self-owned although life is only lent.

In the beating of the pulse
    and the potentials of the mind,
the exaltation of the spirit of the whole of humankind,
it seeks the highest virtue
    while other men are swine before your pearls.
    Welcome to my world.

Welcome to my world,
    it's made of love born out of hating;
with the charcoal from the fire it draws conclusions made of
ash.
The ruins of your dreams become
    the tools for generating
the fleshy scar-tissue that heals the bloody gash.

If I knew where true love came from,
    if that door revealed a crack,
I would volunteer to go, and I would go and not come back.
You who sit there dreaming
    of another pretty girl,
    Welcome to my world.

Welcome to my world,
    it's a temple of the spirit,
where God lives on in exile though the world is sure he's dead;
where your thoughts are free in private,
    you don't need a speaking permit
from the democratic tyrants who don't heed a word you've said.

Here we laugh through all your sermons
　　and we cry through all your jokes,
and no one pays attention to the Rabbis or the Popes.
When the tongues of fire are speaking
　　and the visions are ecstatically unfurled,
　　　　Welcome to my world.

Welcome to my world,
　　it's full of tears but also laughter,
It resides in what is now, it's not concerned with what comes next.
It yearns to hear of grace
　　both before the meal and after,
and it seeks illumination, though it's thoroughly perplexed.

When they write my epitaph,
　　let them praise one thing about me,
that he knew not where the road led, but still dauntlessly he went;
When the wire is barbed and bloody
　　and the sharpest stones are mercilessly hurled,
　　　　Welcome to my world.

*

　　Welcome, indeed. Though the intrusion of the poet is decidedly unprecedented. Bad enough a poet in the 21st century who dares to write in verse, that Ludditism of the Romantic past; but even more scandalous, a poet who augments his text with notes, as though poetry wasn't meant to be obscure!

　　I began writing poetry when I was seventeen, fully believing I was the next Rimbaud, the next Dylan Thomas, the next Walt Whitman. Everything I wrote reflected their works, or whichever other poet I was reading at the time. To write is to give outer form to the inner life; but everything I wrote turned out to have given outer form to someone else's inner life; and worse, in their own words. Eventually, I told myself, eventually I will find my voice, my form. And no doubt eventually I will.

　　In learning how to write, I experimented with every form available to would-be poets: Hebrew piyyut, Japanese Tenka, blank verse, doggerel, the sonnet, the epic, the lyric; and even invented a few forms of my own. The poems selected here bring together the nine volumes that I published privately along the years of my journey: "Early Poems", "Hebrew Poems", "Khaki On Both Sides", "Japanese Poems",

"Coins", "The Pulse", "The Caged Song-Bird of the Muse", "The Strings on the Dome of the Tortoise" and "The Temple and the Word". For those of you who have googled me, and therefore know what I am referring to, some of the "Toronto" poems are included (one was never a poem anyway, but a fragment of my novel "The Flaming Sword"; some I feel inclined to include as an act of defiance, but the truth is, they weren't very good poems in the first place).

Not every poem will come accompanied by a note. In some cases, a mere footnote is sufficient – I have, for many years, found it amusing to seek ways of developing the footnote and the appendix as an aspect of the writing, as an art-form in itself, and in my electronic books you will find I have begun to do the same with the hyperlink: the possibilities for new ways of embracing the word as literature are infinite now that we have the Internet.

Many of the poems printed here are revisions of their former incarnations. As Auden famously reflected, a poem is never finished, but only abandoned. Publishing them in this volume allows me to abandon them again, in some cases entirely, by omitting them, in others by making changes that seem to me improvements. Only four of the poems from "Khaki On Both Sides" have been included, as the remainder require the context of the novel "The Flaming Sword" to be meaningful; poems written for "The Chronicle of the Kingdom of Alphalia", "Going To The Wall" and "The Hourglass" have been excluded in their entirety: entirely pointless to repeat in this volume what is already available in those.

Poetry, as Leonard Cohen once observed, is a verdict, not an occupation. Richard Zenith, in his introduction to Fernando Pessoa's "The Book of Disquiet", judged that "in his poetry he falls short; it isn't sustained like his prose. His poems are the refuse of his prose, the sawdust of his first-rate work." A harsh indictment, but probably true of all prose-writers who happen to write poetry; I include both Wordsworth and Robert Browning. All such judgements about poetry pre-suppose a set of rules that must be followed, a set of expectations that must be adhered to, where the truth is that there are different types of poetry for different moods and purposes; sometimes one wishes to explore a complex idea, at other times simply to capture a passing moment; sometimes the poem is a technical exercise in form and structure, at others a flash of inspiration written down before the Muse changes her mind. Perhaps that is why I feel the need for these notes. Nor is poetry necessarily the expression of the poet's personal opinions, but a rendering into language of a thought, an idea, an experience, a person, a moment, a flower, something that exists in the universe and is amenable to poetical articulation.

3

Genesis

Washed up astounded on the white, white beach
it began - the long, long journey towards
balance. There were the lessons that I learned,
but slowly: careful not to crack the shell,
to slip on stones, to grow my limbs around
the limbs of sea-weed; careful to avoid
the crab-claws and the sideways movements, on
a grey shore, with a storm unwinding, and
my fist closed firmly round the folded pearl.

There were the sea anemones, fractions
of light broken on the sea's mirror; the
round pebbles, round as apples, that I longed
to touch, and clutched; the evanescent name
beyond the Name; the ladders of sea-weed
on which I climbed, stretching my body
and reducing it, stretching the white limbs
upwards and outwards, two unbroken sticks
unbending, two untouching hands unclasping,
two unseeing eyes unveiling, careful to observe.

Within reach of the sun's white candle, I
stood unwavering upon the sand, I
stood unyielding to either cold or heat.
But do not be deceived.
This is not yet balance achieved.
This is just a man, standing on his own two feet.

"Genesis" was published in "Early Poems", in 1981, before home computing had been developed and desk-top publishing was achievable. I ransacked my diaries and notebooks for anything worth looting, and found just fourteen poems, written between 1973 and 1981. Every poem inevitably has its influences; those who like to follow literary tributaries back to their sources will note an affinity in "Genesis" with R.S. Thomas, both in the tone of certain phrases and their vocabulary; simple testimony to the fact that every good writer, whether poet or prosodist, must first and foremost be a versatile and accomplished reader.

Portrait Of A Girl

Outside the window
a juniper moonlight
settles on the lane

Scraped from the shadow
of a rain-swept night
flesh is worn down to grain
of wood and bone

Leaving the empty shape
to haul its hollow weight
across the steps of stones

A car quickly passes
two lights define a shape
transitory gone

Between the grasses
and the closing gate
she leans upon

Then as the curtain opens
shadow and shadow mingle
a footstep sounds on shingle

But only for a moment

Her name was Melanie. She was eighteen and I was twenty-five; far too old for her. Not that I was visiting for love. Her mother served on the committee that was fighting for the Refuseniks, Jews in the Soviet Union who were being persecuted by the authorities for daring to seek permission to emigrate. The moment of the poem happened by chance – an incident of light and sound that I would have loved to capture with a camera, preferably moving, but still would have sufficed. Alas the moment passed, and all that remained was to try to capture it in language.

The Abalone Shell

The afternoon was giving up the struggle,
showers turning to full-fledged rain,
gnats expanding to mosquitoes,
a stone that ripped the plastic flooring of the tent,
the moon flickering like a torchlight behind moving clouds
until it finally succumbed to its own ecliptic darkness.

I made our bed of straw and fallen leaves,
a pillow from my raincoat,
discarded shirts and trousers for a blanket.

So you lay down beside me,
mud on the places
where your clothes had been,
ash between your thighs,
the madness of this assignation by camp-fire
because both of us were young and foolishly romantic
and a hotel would have been profanity and cliché.

We had come - speaking of the sacred -
we had come to Korazim,
the Hill of the Beatitudes where Jesus gave
the Sermon on the Mount,
had come in search of Tabgha,
where two fishes and five loaves fed the incredulous -
unaware the Israelis had moved the site
for the convenience of tourists,
and that Mussolini's Shrine to the Beatitudes
was also just a guess.

But sanctity. Even a wrong site may still be sacred.
Even the profanity of an assignation.
We were piously determined.

*

The abalone shell was an ironic gift,
jewellery fashioned from a sea-snail
that was definitely not kosher

6

yet gave birth to the glorious purple
of the priestly garments.
You wore it around your neck
like a scar where we embraced.
"If I were Christ," I said,
"and you the Magdalene,
I would have given you a crucifix instead".
It wasn't clear what I intended,
but the language and the allusion
were most appropriately irreverent.

You laughed,
kissed the shell,
kissed me,
resumed the struggle.

So we lay,
flesh against flesh
on this hill beneath the moon,
serenaded by air-raid sirens and the
dying fall of bombs,
watched over,
though he probably didn't notice,
by a fighter-pilot parachuting
from a burning plane.

"I accuse you of beauty," you said —
strange words for one who loves,
but these were times when
such an accusation
amounted to an act of civilised behaviour;
only the words were snatched away from us,
by wind kissing the trees,
tussling among rocks,
embracing flower and grass
like the debris of a fallen Mirage-3.

    *

As we rose again,
deep in the valley,
"I accuse you of beauty," you said again.
"Fool!" I replied.

"Don't you know it was I
who commanded the leaves to fall,
my tablets of wind
that smashed against the rocks,
my battalions of poppies
that ruined the plain beauty of this barren field;
my surface to air missile that disproved the mirage?"

So we explored again
the shell's dark magic,
pressing it against your forehead
the way Apache girls do as they greet the sun
on the morning of their initiation into womanhood.
It had to be the abalone shell.
We had intended frankincense and myrrh,
but in your rush you had forgotten it.

Then, suddenly, the moon turned blacker
than the charred debris of the fighter plane
and it was time to leave,
me for night-guard duty,
you to return to base.

"Make love not war," you said,
and winked,
meaning the statement romantically,
but the wink ironically.

The following morning you telephoned in tears
to tell me it was your cousin we had witnessed
parachuting unsuccessfully from the Mirage 3.

The event took place in November 1973, during the Yom Kippur
War, and everything happened just as it is described here. No further
commentary is needed.

Soweto, July 1978

Nothing will remain standing. Not the laws,
not the system, not the white government,
not the BOSS machine, not the policies,
not the bigotry, not the homelands,
not the fine houses, not the parks and stores,
not the monuments to past achievements.
This is a warning and a prophecy:
Nothing, but nothing, will remain standing.

Even your stone houses will not be strong
enough to cover up the cracks, or mute
the sound of gunfire, or hard enough,
or stone enough, to crush your fingers on.
Yet no, the pillars, they will stand upright,
they will support you; all those pillars of
your houses, those of your community -
your pillars will inform posterity.

And they alone will stand, testimony
to a slave empire, the corrupted fruit
of someone else's labour, the fruit that
has produced nothing but a maggot that
will crawl between the pillars, that will cheat
the house of its stability. Then what
will happen to your pillars? Will they wait
for the vindication of History?

The fruit grows wild in the barren garden
of this House of Africa. Wild, but not
yet savage. But when the fingers have been
bandaged, the fingers that you crushed between
the pillars of this stone township, and when
the fingers have been bandaged, and when the
arms and stones have left the slings, how will you
prevent the fingers clenching to a fist?

Rondavel
(Botswana, 1978)

Under this thatched roof
the roundhouse moves in circles -
world without end

    Season upon season I have counted
    the grains of sand that filter through the hourglass
    What was lost or never found - a woman's hand
    her fingers slipping through mine like sand

Give us this day our daily bread

    Sunrise upon sunrise I have watched
    the flowers reawaken after a winter's frost
    The soft ticking of hours and hearts and quills
    names recited to make a pact with History

Teach us this day to receive our daily bread

    I could he says go on like this for ever
    and sometimes I do - in rainy weather

Show us this day how to bake our daily bread

    Because there is no death
    only the breaking of a fragile bond
    the snapping of a brittle chain
    the closing of a wooden box
    changes from light to darkness
    from nothing into one
    then nought again

The bread is baked dry
and History is dumb to every cry
except its own
Harder even than clay
staler than the crumbs of History
these slabs of stone

But these are not death
(for men do not understand death)
these are only
hands drawing apart
a candle guttering
waves breaking on a
sandy
stony
shore

Give us this day Lord water from a stone
Man cannot live by bread alone

There is no returning either
no going back no coming back

And if there is no death
and no returning
who will renew the broken bond
who will provide the yeast for us
to bake in the oven of History?

Life is but a broken arrow
aimed into an aimless future
under this incalculable stone of sky

Lord raise up these crumbs of men
starving in the wilderness
whose pleas fall upon ears of corn
that cannot reap for deafness

"Soweto 1978", "Rondavel" and "Botswana, 1978" belong to a three-month journey, twelve days too many in apartheid South Africa, the rest in the Kalahari desert. I liked the idea of a poem written as a dialogue, even though (perhaps because) the two protagonists here are clearly not listening to each other. The voice of T.S. Eliot can be heard, whispering in the background, though only in the form and language, not the content, which is far too political for him; certainly in the religious content, which he embraced. It should not be necessary to paraphrase a poem into prose, but on this occasion let me say that I envisaged the first voice as Africa, the second as Europe. Forty years after writing it, both are still speaking, both are still not listening.

Botswana, 1978

The first sight of the aloes
reminded me of Israel,
and the first thought of Israel
of a desert and a war.
It is curious the way
experiences fester.

There were no harvests gathered,
no banks were overflowing;
only the barest scrubland
and groups of naked children.
The lightest touch of poetry
would have undermined this starkness.

Their money is called "Pula"
(by those who can afford it).
"Pula" - a Setswana word
meaning simply "may it rain".
Only the poorest people
can spend wishes that freely.

A seminal moment of my life, one Sunday in Sorowe, a village of extreme poverty in which the residents lived in mud huts, and only the government officials lived in brick houses. Plus the priest of course, a European whose small house next to the gorgeous white church was the finest in the village. I attended church that Sunday, and at the end everybody present dropped a Pula into the collection-box, whose purpose was the upkeep of the church. Later I asked my host, who was a development economist, how much it would cost to purchase a dairy cow. The amount he suggested was equivalent to about six months' worth of donations in the collection-box. One dairy cow, I had calculated, could provide all the milk needs of the village, and produce a calf for sale each year; the sale of the calf would purchase a second dairy cow, and every six months another dairy cow, with milk exportable to other villages. Soon enough, in place of a church that declared poverty to be the natural condition of Man as determined by God, economic sustainability could be achieved, and without need of foreign aid.

Nursery School

Notes before the poem, to serve as Virgil to the reader's Dante, or notes after the poem, to serve as Rashi to the reader's Talmud scholar? To experiment with a new form is to raise questions never previously asked. Where law and science insist on single answers, absolutes, I am content with multiple possibilities. On this occasion, the guiding hand seems to me necessary, because context changes everything and this was written in a very specific context: the summer of 1983, the summer after the War of Peace for Galilee in which the PLO was expelled from Lebanon and the massacre of Palestinian refugees took place in the Beirut camps of Sabra and Shatila; when I was teaching in a kibbutz school in Israel and paid a visit to a Palestinian school on the West Bank. But perhaps the context is not everything. Had circumstances been different, I could have written the same poem in Soweto or Johannesburg in 1978, and could write it today in Isfahan, in Lyon, in Tripoli, in Baltimore, in Liverpool, in Melbourne, and sadly, still, in Israel.

On the wall a geography of bones
teaches of mother earth and father land,
its body prostrate, supine, an effigy
of some dead patriarch or ancient hero
mummified in time, embalmed in history,
preserved relic of our shared identity.

The tongue is silent that once spoke the roots
of words we speak; the fleshless corpse is naked
that once dressed as we still dress,
and dreamed, and grew embittered
with the self-same disappointments. This body
(its wrist-tag bearing the wrong name)
a rib-cage of grids and contours;
eyes of lakes; breasts of hills;
limbs and members severed by the surgery of war;
the deep declension of the pelvis meaning valley;
the splayed fingers surrendering a tattered flag,
the mute lips on which an anthem died,
and there (say nothing, pretend not to have seen,
leave unexplained, except rhetorically,

in metaphor) the love bite, the mons pubis,
the future generations lying impotent between.

In the barren fields beyond the school -
land being once again reclaimed, reconquered -
the cactuses are flowering,
whole tracts of desert bloom and blossom
under the falling manna of a night's dull rain.
Dry grass turns green as mould,
swamp and river deepen into drowning pools:
life and death eternally recycled,
the one into the other, and then back again.

Here, we look at earth and see its history,
growing from the soil upwards and outwards:
bone of tree, flesh of flower,
(human degeneration, whether into corpse or killer)
the great necropoloi, the tombstone cities we bedeck
with flowers and inscriptions of ancestor-worship;
and the new cities, rising out of bog or ruin,
plaster white as calcified bones,
clay brown as coagulated blood or poisoned liver,
growing death out of a corpse of land,
grafting history upon history, layer by layer
like living archaeological remains -
but the nursery children are clamouring for games.

In school they teach us how to love selectively,
not for who we are,
but for which side we are on,
not for good unless "our" good,
nor evil unless "their" evil,
not for human,
but for race, class, nation, colour, gender,
learning love by learning who to hate.

Thus the map of our common greed and selfishness,
our flag, our anthem, our tribe, our party,
our collective alibi for xenophobia,
our shared impunity in justifying cruelty,
our connubial blanket of barbed wire,
our walls, our guards, our laws, our customs -
walls that keep us in and keep you out.

There are, of course, atrocities on both sides,
breaches of the civilised codes of killing,
the humanitarian norms of genocide in war,
the same rhetoric used to praise or to condemn.
There are, on both sides, broken bones, exploding
bullets - but this, this is the worst atrocity:
children re-assembling matchstick flags,
designing egg-box parliaments,
learning by heart the nobility of the cause,
reciting by rote the names of kings and martyrs,
creating their Blue Peter liturgies of heroines
and heroes, singing the anthem, saluting the flag,
in all their four-year innocence.

This, this is the worst atrocity,
this process of indoctrination,
this teaching of conflict, antagonism, hate,
this idealism of the moderate middle-classes,
this preaching of the moral libertarians,
this all-justifying dream of peace, equality,
harmony, democracy – teachers, nurses, parents
massaging the unset foetal jelly
of cerebral muscle, softening it up,
loosening its sphincters, each thumbpress
bearing down upon the nerve of inhumanity,
not to heal, nor soothe, as masseuses do,
but stretching the brain upon the rack of ideology
until it is remoulded in the image of its own
destruction, and growing to maturity it bears
forever
the scar-tissue of imparted love-through-hate
that dribbles from its lips like mother's milk
all in the name of truth and right and good.

This, this is the worst atrocity.
Barren fields will grow again, and die, and be reborn.
Corpses will rot till flowers bloom in them.
Desert will turn to bog and bog to desert.
Eternity will tussle in the arms of death
and give birth to eternity.
All that is nothing - merely nothing.
But this, this is the terrible something,

far worse than broken bones, or ropes, or bombs,
this disfiguring of a child's heart and mind,
this breaking of a child's humanity,
this, this process of indoctrination,
this is the ultimate atrocity,
perpetrated by each side
against itself.

The notion that learning poetry by heart will improve the memory is as meaningless as suggesting that reading books will improve the eyesight or that listening to music will make a deaf man hear again. We exercise our physical muscles in order to make them stronger, because we know that the alternative – a sedentary laziness – will allow them to atrophy. But this is not true of the memory, which is in constant use, even unconsciously. The truth is, teachers require children to memorise poetry because they don't really know what else to do with poetry in the classroom, and parents, even if not all children, like to encourage the act of showing off, which can be achieved by reciting poetry out loud. If the goal is to aid children in understanding poetry, then it is necessary first to provide instruction in the techniques of poetry, to explain onomatopoeia and alliteration and simile and metaphor, in much the same way that integers and quadratic equations are explained in maths class, and neutrons and black holes in physics; this however makes for extremely dull and sterile English lessons, and tends to put children off poetry. Writing a poem out by hand, and in your neatest handwriting, engages the intellect at a deeper level of cognition, allowing the brain to hear the rhythms and the cadences more clearly, to gauge the changes of tone; this is a useful exercise for the classroom, though also very boring. Learning a poem by heart can potentially achieve the same, provided that the person doing the memorising is actually focusing on the meaning of the words they are absorbing, though sadly this rarely takes place. Poetry represents the use of language at its highest and its deepest form, and the canon of world poetry is one of the greatest human contributions to civilisation; and yet, today, few publishers will publish it, because nobody is reading it. Until we fathom how to teach it interestingly, this will not change.

The River

Straight from the mountain
downwards flows the river
strong and fresh and clear

straight towards the valley
it flows downwards
until

convinced by its own arguments
  the river
bends

Grey it flows through the grey world
  dark through these dark cities
    sheltering under rocks and bridges
      hiding beneath flowers
        seeking its refuge in the open sea

It loves its own reflections
  which make of it a pool
    for its own looking and laughing

It loves to lie down in green valleys
  to sleep and make a bed for reeds
    to dance around the saplings
      and the summer trees

It loves the dialogues of fishermen
  played out patiently and long
    To catch or not to catch
trickling its own dialogues over a duck's back

Yet
     how
          like
       a
snake
     it crawls!

These mountains are too steep
  it does not even dare or try
    to climb beyond itself
      towards these icy heights

Tell it to rise upwards – it moves not
Tell it to stop flowing – it hears not
Tell it to swim against the current – it can not

Downwards it flows
  ever downwards

straight from the mountain
downwards flows the river
strong and fresh and clear

straight into the valley
it flows downwards
until

convinced by its own arguments
  the river
bends

Fairy Tale

Caterpillar on a leaf
in a torpid state of disbelief
turned into a chrysalis
and studied how to fly

While I upon my futile legs
in a wasted hour learned to beg
then spread my arms towards the sun
and studied how to cry

The Meal

Once a wild beast lurked in wilder bushes
to stalk his prey: horn stuck (like a pig!) through
fleshy grass, reaching, pulling, tearing
at his meal, blood-raw tongue licking at the dew
on lips by dawn twice breakfasted - then claw
mauling, teeth chiselling, ravenous jawbone
crunching once life into always death: stone
death.

   Or so it was once - but is no more.

Now, here, is dead fact, not living fiction:
domesticated man in smock and bib,
dressing the lame beast of women's lib,
chopping vegan salad in the kitchen.

   This was one of the "Toronto" poems, and what more innocent
little victim was ever scapegoated in the long history of witch-hunts?
I understood the malice and the mischievousness and the egotism of
the witch-hunters, but I never did understand why this was included
in the list of the supposedly heretical, blasphemous, scandalous and
otherwise depraved. The complaint of the witch-hunters was that it
was misogynistic, which I can only take as a complete failure to
understand the poem. The complaint of the poem is not against
women at all, but against those men whose response to women's lib
is total and abject surrender, a response that is equally as useless to
the women as it is to the men.

The Song Of Sisyphus

I have called this poem "The Song of Sisyphus". In the Jewish tradition in which I grew up, the word "shir" may stand for either poetry or song, and may be recited musically or prosaically, with or without accompanying instruments. Reading King David's Psalms, for example, the distinction is just as blurred between verse and prose. I have written many songs for guitar and piano or even full rock or jazz band, but only one of those, "Welcome To My World", is included in this collection, and that because it was written as a poem first, then set to music.

For those unfamiliar with the myth, Sisyphus was punished for cursing the gods; his sentence, to push a large boulder to the summit of a tall mountain, from where the gods would then project it back to the bottom, and he required to clamber down and push it up again. A perfect analogy for the "absurdity" of the human condition, according to the French philosopher Albert Camus. My version amends the Greek original to my own philosophical position, one which refuses to collaborate in its own victimhood. I am also conscious that the crucial word-play on the word "dam" is likely to be untranslatable.

> In these days of my dying I have come back to the
>   mountain, a man bred on sluggish rivers,
> taught to unwind whatever stream and pour it gently,
>   gratefully, slipping over rocks,
> taught to lie down on soft, dry beds, to tend the
>   trees and flowers, to know my limits and to keep
>   within my boundaries,
> taught to look upwards to the peaks and shield my
>   eyes against the blinding light of suns, of gods,
>   of madmen, who alone could travel there,
> taught to look upwards and admire, even while my back
>   bent downwards to the long, flat sea,
> taught to obey the flowing of the current, to brace
>   myself against the cold, to spin only where the
>   whirlpool turned me, to cease when I faced the
>   overpowering
>   dam.

And when I reached the sea, I found a ragged shell,

and opened it, I probed its ache of darkness,
    tampering, discarding, modifying, uncovering
      its broken body piece by piece,
        and keeping, or not keeping.
I took the half-made shell and plunged it deep into
    the acid of its dissolution, and reformed it,
      moulding its darkness with my own bare hands,
        until it was complete.

And then I held it to the skies, my head turned
    upwards to the mountain-tops, the tiny god I had
      created gleaming in my hands, my own pride gleaming,

as I raised my head and laughed,
as I raised my voice and cursed,
as I raised my idol to the sun
    and threw it like a rock into the river.

Oh, it was ambitious, it was brazen, but I was always
    ambitious, I who found the river far too sluggish, I
      who knew that nothing could be safe or simple that a
        man made in defiance of his gods.

But I had touched the unknown, and touching I had
    learned it was not God.
But I had reached into the darkness, and clutching I
    had learned it was not Hell.
But I had pierced the invisible, and seeing I had
    learned I was not blind.

There are mysteries, moments of pure magic, there are
    revelations, visions in a dream of dissipated light,
      there are heights beyond the mountain-tops,
and these too I have found, and held,
    and formed with my own hands, yet never once
      did my feet lift off the earth, never once
        did I fail to soar beyond the clouds.

Thus did I live, and now, in these days of my dying,
    I have come back to the mountain, a man bred on
      sluggish rivers, a man prepared to lift the rock and
        hoist it upwards to the peaks, to stand there, my

head tilted skywards, my eyes unshielded,
my voice raised to the gods,

as I curse them
as I defy them,
as I lift the rock upon my shoulders, and hurl it,
as I once hurled an idol I had made
  into the paltry river,
    into the weak and flimsy,
      quickly-broken
      dam.

G.K. Chesterton once remarked, with his tongue firmly pressed to his cheek, that "The poets have been mysteriously silent on the subject of cheese". There are, in fact, more than 700 known cheeses in the world, alphabetically from Abbaye de Belloc all the way to Gorgon Zola, and including along the way such deliciously poetic names as Acapella, Balaton, Bandal, Bishop Kennedy, Bocconcini, Brebis du Lavort, Burgos, Cantal, Crowley, Danbo, Daralagjazski, Derby, Fin de Siècle (admittedly an epoch of poetry and not a form or a poet), Fontainebleau, Galbani, Gowrie, Goya, Hervé, Humboldt (or at least his creator, Nabokov), Lappi (Lippi was a painter, though celebrated in a famous poem by Robert Browning), Leafield, Leyden, Loch Arthur (I am including the epics), Little Rydings (omitted, presumably by mistake, from the "Four Quartets") Llanboidy, Malvern (which is in Worcestershire, while Marlow is in Buckinghamshire), Passendale (correctly spelled Passchendaele in Belgium; world war one poets by the dozen), Podhalanski, Port Nicholson (the port may be moot, though he was known to enjoy a dram), Pont l'Eveque (not clear which Bishop but several come to mind, from George Berkeley to the American Poet Laureate Elizabeth), Processed Cheddar (rather too much of that, in the anthologies especially), Romano, Roncal (troubadour verse), Roquefort, Roumy, Rubens (I am thinking of the great Nicaraguan Ruben Dario, and Dylan's masterpiece about Rubin Carter, but neither match the spelling; Goethe's "Prometheus" fits the bill, music by Schubert, painting by Rubens), Saga, Saint-Andre, Sirene (a cheese that whispers and a taste that drives men to the rocks), Sonoma Jack (legendary blues artist, great lyrics), Wookey Hole (the original Cheddar, and of course Coleridge's "caverns measureless to man", Wensleydale (see Wordsworth) and many others, too many to list. It seems to me the poets have not been silent at all on the subject of cheese; nor cheese, in the matter of poetry.

Talismans

Certain simple chord progressions
strummed softly on a Spanish guitar

The sudden shift of mood that coincides
with sunset and the fall of evening

The contact of flesh on flesh
speaking more eloquently than language

The sands of the desert stretching to eternity
mile upon mile of mile upon mile

Books that take on magical properties
for the number of times
you have failed to solve their riddles

The movement of sunlight
on water glass skin

Talismans

Moments that yield to the clutching hand
or to poetry
or to nothingness

I wrote, a page or two ago, that only one of my songs had made its
way into this collection. That is only partially accurate. Several poems
became the starting-points for songs much later on; this was one of
them.

Unemployed

I write to pass the time
though almost any other occupation
would be preferable

Still
a man has to do something
to convince himself
that he is not alone

I am not alone
I am one of three million slaves
locked in most curious brotherhood
unable to find a real set of chains

It was the spring of 1981. I had obtained both my Bachelor's and Master's degrees and thought I wanted to be an actor. For several months I lived with my parents and worked with a fringe theatre company, until it became obvious that neither of these situations had any future to them. The worst unemployment crisis in British history was, though few would admit it, a deliberate strategy of the Thatcher government, the wilful destruction of the entire manufacturing and industrial base of the UK, in part to destroy the power of the unions, in part to bring the vile politics of Ronald Reagan to Britain, the cult of Ayn Rand which is the apotheosis of narcissism, the rejection of "society" in favour of the "individual", the abandonment of the altruism and humanitarianism on which Judeo-Christian civilisation had been built. So right wing was this government, the threat posed previously by those wannabe fascists the National Front and the British National Party disappeared. Conscious that what was needed was a revolution, but that the disaster of Cromwell and the Commonwealth meant the British would never again embark on such a course, I enjoyed seeing my letter on the subject of unemployment published in "The Times", then packed my rucksack and made aliya to Israel.

And yes, I agree with you, there is something questionable, though whether about the poem or the commentary is not so obvious, about a poem whose commentary is longer than the poem itself.

Easter Sunday

If nothing else today
at least the sun has risen
and if not to the Father
than into the white sepulchral morning

And you my brothers
when will you rise up
when will you put on the crown of thorns
and loose the chains that bind you to the Cross?

The Condemned Man

The death cell is quiet; my
breakfast has been cleared away,
as has the unwanted priest.
Now begins the real trial,
entered with full conviction.
I know that I shall pass. I
know that none has failed yet.

Actually, it isn't true. Many have been committed to the electric
chair, the gallows, the auto-da-fé, lethal injection, firing squad, the
guillotine, a hundred other instruments of judicial murder invented
by mere humanity (including the cross alluded to in "Easter
Sunday"), and survived because the mechanism failed. God, on the
other hand, despite the delusion of his devotees that he regards all
human life as sacred, may extend the time allotted, but has never
yet failed to make the mechanism work effectively.

Portrait Of A Man

With the exception of the poem about Kurt Waldheim, which was added later, the next set of poems, from the collection "Hebrew Poems", belongs to the three and a half years I spent in Israel in the early 1980s, my second extended stay there, until my second extended disillusionment drove me back again to England. The first, "Portrait Of A Man", was intended for Ari Ben Aaron, the hero of my novels "The Flaming Sword" and "A Little Oil & Root", written in Israel at this time.

First there is the name –
which I shall not mention –
skewered on the tongue's forked blade
Then there is the man himself
the swatch of bone and tissue
the veil of flesh
the tattoo numbered on one forearm
the scar marked above one eye
the weary movement of a broken arm across
the swung pendulum of a conversation
the trembling in the hollow of a thigh

This – all this – and nothing:
the rumours bartered in the market-place
the fictions and disguises
the transitory syllogism of the ego
the indecipherable hieroglyphs
carved on a face of stone

By a certain bridge
where I have often seen him
I watch his shadow in the lamplight
and his image in the water
trying to unlock the symbols
of an unknown algebra

Apotheosis

They carried me to Egypt and made a slave of me,
squared my beard, curved the fringes of my hair,
dressed me in the clothes of an Egyptian -
till I was nothing more than wood and stone,
incense on an altar, fire in an olive tree,
a drunken feast, a brother's love for sister,
a timid shackle and a foul abomination.

See how they cowered before some human face,
calling it my face, naming it my name,
horror in their hearts and bowels mingling
with my own horror at such vile degradation,
my humiliation in their midst, a slave of slaves,
proud nakedness reduced to clothed indignity,
my loins bound with cord, my blood sapped by labour,
my will tethered like a rooster in its chains.

But will will be done, and done will be proven.
For their sakes I threw down the puny idols,
threw off the human mask, threw back the chains,
tormented my tormentors with some easy plagues,
cast some simple miracles into their midst,
bent back my wings and soared into the freedom
of the desert - for their sakes, not for mine.

Come, my children -
now, at last, to live and grow,
now to forge a will of iron
stronger than any shackle.

What of the sea - I who have turned back
whole firmaments? The sea parted like a harlot's
thighs submitting to my rod of iron.

What of the desert - I who have made
worlds out of voids? The desert is already dust.

What of the hordes pursuing? Come, my children!
Could Sodom or Gomorrah stand against me?

Desert of blistering heat, waterless, foodless;
desert of ice cold night, woodless for a fire;
desert of endless space, caveless for a refuge -
come, my children, I shall feed you,
my blood shall quench your thirst,
my love shall nourish you,
my body light your journey,
my spirit be for you a sanctuary.
Each of you with my own hand
I shall smuggle out of bondage -
tell it to your children,
how with my own hand I warmed and nourished you,
lit your way,
made of my spirit a sanctuary for your spirits.

Though others tried to supersede me,
none had forged a will like mine,
and one by one they fell before me,
melting in the sun like golden calves.
Enemies I brushed aside.
Rivals were crushed beneath my fist.
Fear lit up my children's eyes - fear and reverence.
How they longed to learn the secrets of the fire!

Do not look at me - I burn.
Do not touch me - I consume.
Do not question me -
I too have learned to fear the fire.

Faceless, my flesh assumed the spirit of the fire,
flame by day, ember smouldering by night,
lighting the journey like a reflection of my will.

In stone I carved a law so harsh and so implacable
that only such as I could possibly obey it.
In sand I forged my children,
turning slaves to soldiers, peasants into priests.

Who would dare to know me?
Who would dare to stand before me?
Are you strong enough, bold enough, vigorous enough?
I too would fear to stand before me.

Then will you wrestle with me, Israel,
here on this high mountain
where Israel wrestled with me?

Those who come cowering I blow away like chaff,
those who come snivelling I spit upon,
those who come kneeling I make to grovel.

Will you wrestle with me, Israel,
here on this broken ladder
where Israel wrestled with me?
I too would fear the iron in the fist.

Strong enough to survive my desert,
to endure my fire;
arrogant enough to pierce my cloak invisible;
man enough to look and touch and live;
ready enough to fight or be consumed.
Why are you limping, Israel? I have not yet
touched the hollow of your thigh,
I have not yet put it out of joint.
Come, my children, wrestle with me,
thigh for thigh, ladder for ladder, fear for fear.

At the edge of the abyss I made judges
out of prisoners, lawyers out of liars, warriors
out of snivelling children. In the craters
of volcanoes I forged giants out of dwarves.
In the trembling of an earthquake
my own voice trembled,
and I shattered every idol who contended with me.
Come, my children, answer - are you worthy of me?

Which of you is capable of envisaging Paradise,
of marching towards it sword in hand,
conquering it, inhabiting it,
building my palace for eternity?

What - did you expect me to take you by the hand
and lead you over Jordan like some shepherd?
Where are your swords, my children?
Where are your teeth, sharpened on paschal lamb?

Where is your will of iron,
wrought in the desert fire and in my iron will?
Must I destroy the sheep as I destroyed the calf?

Climb to the fiery summit of your soul
and wrestle with me, Israel, will to will.
I have made my children strong enough to wrestle,
I have taught my children the arrogance of fire,
I have formed my children in my own likeness,
limping not from the chains they drag behind,
but from the undefeated agony of a dislocated thigh.

I am a rod of flaming iron,
a lion who leaves the sheep-pen bloody,
a flame invisible searing the dark night,
a white moon gleaming out of deepest nothingness.

I am, as this desert made me.
I am - that I am.
Come, my children.
Children, Israel, wrestle.

Two ironies emerge from this poem, neither of which I was aware of when I wrote it. The first is the inference of the necessity of exterior struggle to complement the inner struggle: the inevitability and inexorability of armed conflict when the exterior struggle is about geography, tribal rivalry, political disagreement, economics. The second is the translation of both the word and the concept of "struggle", complete with the above inference, into Arabic; for in Arabic the word is Jihad.

A Poem Of Sarah

Isaac, my child, my only child,
your father would have killed you
had the Lord not stayed his hand,
willingly he would have killed you,
for his covenant is writ in blood.

Isaac, my child, my only child,
see how your father stands each night
in the doorway of his tent,
counting the stars of heaven
like a proud father.

The Tablets

Half-way down the mountain
Moses stopped abruptly
catching his mind upon a thought
like a foot upon an unseen rock

Had he been younger
and more energetic
he might have gone back again
and demanded Justice

But he did not

He dropped the tablets
on which the Laws were carved

for in his hands
they had already turned to stone

The Ballad Of The Master-Builders
A Song For Children

In the days when we were slaves in Eden
We built the first great myth of God
Founding all the world's religions
Sowing the first seed in the sod

    We are the Jews a desert people
    Forty generations cast out on the sands
    We are the Jews the master-builders
    Building monuments on other people's lands

Then when we were slaves in Egypt
Selling our souls for the highest bid
We carried the rocks from Ismailia
And built the first great pyramid

    We are the Jews a desert people
    Forty generations cast out on the sand
    We are the Jews the master-builders
    Building monuments on other people's lands

When we were slaves in Nero's Rome
And the people demanded a panacea
We tore down the walls of our holy Temple
And built for them the Coliseum

    We are the Jews a desert people
    Forty generations cast out on the sands
    We are the Jews the master-builders
    Building monuments on other people's lands

Later still enslaved in Europe
We built the first great banking systems
Our prophets Einstein Marx and Freud
Laid the foundations of modern wisdom

We are the Jews a desert people
Forty generations cast out on the sands
We are the Jews the master-builders
Building monuments on other people's lands

And now that we are free in Israel
We build a state of discontent
Building farms from sand and marshes
Building towns and settlements

We are the Jews a desert people
Forty generations cast out on the sands
We are the Jews the master-builders
Building monuments on other people's lands

"Hebrew Poems" was privately published in 1984. It wasn't available to purchase in shops, but somehow a copy reached the editor of the Jewish Chronicle, who passed it to a reviewer, who wrote just a single line, at the end of a review of someone else's poems. No mention of anything else in the collection; simply a hostile-defensive remark about this poem, suggesting that I must be some kind of self-hating Jew for writing it, and even more so for publishing it. The kind of criticism that is taught in "Nursery School".

To Kurt Waldheim, Christmas 1987

Dear Mr Waldheim I will keep my letter brief
As I know you are a very busy man
For you have finished up as the great white chief
While I am merely scrapings in a van

Dear Mr Waldheim I'm sure it isn't true
All those awful things they say about your youth
As President of Austria it simply wouldn't do
If those libels should turn out to be the truth

Dear Mr Waldheim I don't think you should resign
After all you were just some bureaucrat
You were just obeying orders and following the line
There is surely nothing criminal in that

Dear Mr Waldheim, I was really glad to hear
Your Christmas message of goodwill to all
In response I write to wish you a prosperous New Year
And hope to see you sometime in the fall

Dear Mr Waldheim I am really at a loss
To send this letter or to let it burn
For you have run the UN and been Austria's boss
But me I'm only ashes in an urn

Secretary-General of the United Nations from 1972 to 1981, he was
elected President of Austria in 1986, despite international controversy
over the revelation that he had served as an intelligence officer in the
Wehrmacht during World War II.

A Sentimental Poem
Discussing The Much-Vexed Question Of
Identity

Who is a Jew? I will answer you –
 but let us not speak of gods,
  let us speak only in human terms,
   since to God there is no question.

A Jew is a soul longing for Jerusalem.

A Jew is a shield raised in defence
 of the land of his forefathers:
  Korazim, Gaza, Jericho.

A Jew is roots that go down
 deeper than the Hula valley,
  deeper than the Sharon Rose,
   into three thousand years of bedrock.

A Jew is belonging to the land he has tilled,
 above Galilee and below the Negev.

A Jew is the children he has buried
 in millennia of conquest and invasion.

A Jew is claiming the land of Canaan
 because he has no other home;
  driven from land to land,
   hounded into camps and ghettos,
    persecuted, massacred,
     rejected and forsaken.

Who is a Jew? I will answer you –
 all of these things make a man a Jew,
  and if not a Jew,
   then a Palestinian.

Elijah

I watched an eagle soar through proud but vacant skies
 until my eyes grew stiff with studying
  and then I fixed my gaze on it
   and froze it there

The way was obvious - forward through the marshes
 forward over Pisgah and the Jordan
  down through Jericho and Moriah to
   Jerusalem

But the axe that I carried had turned blunt on me
 and fragile futile as a memory
  frozen like an eagle hovering
   an eagle with its wings clipped by the sun

   Before the shadow sets
   Before the desert grows too cold
   Before these stones have hardened
   Before the city on the sands
   Before the wise men call me arid

I travelled slowly over stubborn empty sands
 until my hands grew stiff with grovelling
  and then I fixed my gaze upon the town
   and wandered there

The path was wide and winding - stumbling over rocks
 stumbling over stones of words
  carrying them on towards Zion towards
   Jerusalem

But the voice I had borrowed had turned dry on me
 a voice of stone in an arid desert
  on a loose tongue in a parched mouth
   through a dead land

As the shadow falls
As the desert grows and gathers
As the hearts turn stony
As the city fills with fools
As the wise men call me

The lawyers argued with me loud but hollow words
  until their thoughts grew stiff with arguing
   and then they fixed their gaze upon me
    and cursed me there

The road was blocked with soldiers - over the rough stones
  with the rough stones at my back - over the hills
   and onward to Gehenna from
    Jerusalem

But the fruit I had gathered had turned sour on me
  and lingered in the mouths of caves
   the hollow mouths the hollow caves
    the stone symbols of these feet of clay

  When the shadow lengthens
  When the desert turns to dust
  When the hearts have hardened
  When the city sleeps
  When the wise men call

    Remember

  Stone breaking stone with stone
  Leeches clinging on the backs of leeches

    Remember

A Poem Of Protest
To The Colloquium on Jewish Literature
March 1984

In Jewish Quarterly Volume 31, Nos 3/4 - the "old Jews" declared that the "new Jews" could not and should not write about either the Holocaust or the Exile, experiences they had not had and therefore could not properly comprehend. This poem was submitted as a "Letter to the Editor", but never published.

On the day that I came out of darkness
Holocaust was History,
Diaspora defunct,
Exile ended,
the stage at Auschwitz swept and emptied,
the poems of Isaiah returned to literature
by half a generation wanting,
half a generation fearing,
to forget,
or simply to misremember.

On that day was Ha Levi's sanctuary
half rebuilt, and Ibn Ezra's dream already
turning sour among the dunes and wadis
and the bee-infested combs and coombes.
I grew up learning about
citrus groves and Bergen-Belsen, about
Delilah's hairdressing salon, about
Mengele's dental surgery, about
Dreyfus and the Shabtai Zvi, about
the wisdom with which Solomon decreed partition.
And it was all just history.
I hadn't been there.
I hadn't lived through it.
I had neither died nor - worse - survived.
My hands were clean,
my heart untorn,
my conscience untroubled -
what business of mine was any of this?

How could I write about it then,
exiled in the English language
that I only half believed in,
speaking Hebrew in Mizrachic drawl,
uncertain of exact meanings in my translations
of Nachmann and Givrol and Bashevis Singer?

History was a stage for scholarship,
to be reviewed, critically or uncritically,
whether in newspaper or in Midrash.

And because I came out of the wrong darkness,
because I acted upon the wrong stage,
because I studied the wrong documents,
because I did not experience the events,
because I did not hold the bequest,
but only the inheritance,

because God brought me out of Egypt,
and out of Babylon,
and out of Bergen-Belsen.

Time Immemorial

Time has not taught men much
beating against eternity
like a panic-stricken bird
lashing the cruel stroke of midnight

Who now remembers the dry white stones
the thorns the thongs the cacti
and how the souls of our fathers
were given up each to its own desert?

Ah but now the season opens
fresh as poppies white as dead men's bones
earth grows its harvest of summer fruit
sea has not spilled over.

Who at this equinox will taste my fever
these hands that quake
these eyes that burn?
Who will count the changes of the inner clock?

Listen: my skin is made of lampshades
my heart is made of rainbow
my blood is milk and honey -
which of you will taste my promise?

The bodies of men make strong manure
See these poppies that were once Akiva
this cactus that was once Bar Kochba
The pyramid of Ramesses is strewn with ivy

No time has not taught much
nor time nor history
men do not hear the prayers
exploding in the synagogues

Nor taught nor learned
the clocks still toll the minutes
the bone-white sand still fills
the desert's hourglass

The sign upon my house still reads:
"Here lives a Jew"

I have never understood the need to "define" poetry, to say what it is, and I suspect that all definitions are necessarily fanciful, which is apposite, as it is that most fanciful of all human inventions, poetry, which is being defined. Some of my favourites are below:

To be a poet is a condition, not a profession. – Robert Frost

Poetry is just the evidence of life. If your life is burning well, poetry is just the ash. — Leonard Cohen

Poetry is the journal of a sea animal living on land, wanting to fly in the air. — Carl Sandburg

The poet is the priest of the invisible. — Wallace Stevens

A poet's work is to name the unnameable, to point at frauds, to take sides, start arguments, shape the world, and stop it going to sleep. – Salman Rushdie

For what is a poem but a hazardous attempt at self-understanding: it is the deepest part of autobiography. – Robert Penn Warren

A poet is, before anything else, a person who is passionately in love with language. — W.H. Auden

Stigma-Stigmata
A Poem For My Christian Friends

You told me to turn the other cheek
I turned it
You slapped me
Again and again
Told
     Turned
          Slapped
Till the flesh on my cheeks
Turned into scabs

Now you are sorry
And want me to turn a cheek of friendship
But you are still the one who gives the orders
And I am still the one who must comply
Now turn one cheek
Now turn the other cheek
There - we have kissed and made up

But nothing has really changed
Except the smack of palm for smack of lips
Smack of the Jesus-slap
Smack of the Judas-kiss
And the scabs upon my cheeks
Where the flesh will not grow back

A number of my Jewish friends have expressed concern over this poem, because they are committed to what is known as "the interfaith dialogue". I refer them to my essay, "A Timeline of Christian Anti-Semitism", and to a poem later in this collection (see page 182), "Vergangenheitsbewältung", which describes a process known in post-apartheid South Africa as "Truth and Reconciliation". When the Christian church finally faces up to the Truth, and begins the process of Redemption and Reparations, when Christians recognise the offense caused by wearing around their necks the icon of a murdered Jew, then and only then will I be ready to discuss Reconciliation.

Prayer

Blessed art thou, Lord of separation,
who created this unbroken silence,
created worlds for us to be apart,
created absence, created distance,
made this great ache of longing in my heart.
Blessed, for that very separation,
casts me back upon my deepest self, tests
me, makes me mine my own resources, be
sufficient, whole and individual;
and in that very act of casting, then,
Lord, then, your absence draws me in again.
Grant me, Lord, forever, your eternal
blessed ache of separation. Grant me,
Lord, forever, this drawing to your breast.

Elegy On The Death Of Moses

Alone in this bleak desert, under a cold moon,
on the dry hill-slopes with the mosquitoes preying,
and the fire cracking its knuckles brighter than any
revelation - the laws of time carved on a face of
stone whose lips now barely stammered their last song,
and eyelids stuttered wearily in closing upon sleep.

No time now. Desert had consumed his vision,
sunk it in quicksand, blinded him with mirages.
Too long following the cloud of smoke had left
his legs directionless. Authority had stooped his
back and no commandment had ordained for him a
litter. On the barren rock-face of his life's pyramid,
no mark, no covenant, only the sand-scratched,
abstract image and the shadow of an unseen likeness,
uniting all divinity in a time-bound rib of dust.

So he sat, on the curved tooth of the hill, waiting.
The tongues of fire had licked his vision clean,
manna had failed to satisfy his hunger, age had paled
his bones, and now his stick upon the rock could
bring forth only silence. Though he had dreamed
of milk and honey, spoken the unspeakable, roamed
more high and widely even than the Bedou, though he
had found the path and paved it, measured out the
weights and balances, numbered every head, though he
had tripped and stumbled bravely to the very summit
of the mountain - here, now, was the end of time.
For Pisgah, it seems, is about as far
as a man may reasonably hope to travel.

It could have been the end of all time - now and
ever. Forty years had slipped through his fingers,
like grains of sand, like a woman's fingers.
Embers now the burning bush, skinless the serpent
from the rod, parched the desert's mouth, dried up
the rock's drawn water, gone the sea's parting.
Apparently there had been some sin, some crime,
once - it was so hard to remember - an act in

anger, or defiance, some such, a brass serpent or
a golden bull-calf, one of the six hundred and
thirteen commandments no doubt - who could possibly
remember let alone obey so many harsh and complicated
edicts? - some ritual impurity perhaps, touching the
unwritten laws, impinging on His jealousy; some sin,
some crime, but truly he could not remember.

Only how he had waved farewell, confident in his
successor, wishing he could part the waters
of the Jordan as a last gift to his people
who could not know about the waiting war,
the broken promise.

                    Yet he knew.
In the sands' riddle he had prophesied disillusion.
In the stars' arcana he had predicted the judgements
of posterity. Men dream the last oasis. Yet so many
years of wilderness had taught him to expect mirages.
So he listened, and heard - only the desert's voice,
sighing in the wind like crickets. So he looked,
and saw - only the landscape of his life,
flatter than any desert.

And unable to remember what sin, what crime,
he wondered why he had been left behind, abandoned
on this hillside overlooking Jordan. Was it simply
that he had done his work, simply that he had
grown too old, simply to spare him from the bleaker
desert that persisted beyond stream and mountain?

Alone in this bleak desert, under a cold moon,
on the dry hill-slopes with the mosquitoes preying -
a passing stranger might have noticed an old sad
man, scratching with his fingers in the dust,
listening to the desert hush and the crack
of embers, seeing in the fading fire
the miracle of his own death.

The Plaint Of Rachel

Is it really so remarkable that a man came to a well
and met a woman who he found attractive?
I came to the same well.
I found a man attractive.
Yet my coming does not even earn a paragraph.

Is it really so extraordinary that a man waited
seven years to obtain his love,
and slaved, and counted every minute,
only to be cheated at the last?
I also waited seven years, and slaved,
and counted every minute.
I also was cheated at the last.
Yet my disappointment does not even merit a sentence.

Is it really so historic that a man continued waiting,
adding another seven years,
fleeing at the last?
Did I stop waiting?
Did my feet not also burn the dust in flight?
Yet my determination is not even worth a mention.

Your story will be told, my husband, my patriarch.
Your story will require whole chapters.
Yet I who shared your longing, your dream, your bed,
my name would not even be remembered
if I had had the same patience
for another man.

A plaint is an utterance of grief or sorrow, a lamentation. A complaint is an expression of dissatisfaction, pain, uneasiness, censure or resentment. The two words come from the same root and are remarkably similar, yet also subtly different, and it is very sad that the former has virtually disappeared from the English language, save only its misuse in the word plaintiff, which should really be a complaintiff. This note, on the other hand, is both a plaint and a complaint.

The Song Of The Wandering Jew

Homeless as a Jew
I map the sedentary exile of a mortgaged room,
shed the stadtl of my thoughts' diaspora,
burst the ghetto-gates of my imagination -
then pack my few belongings in a trunk of verse
and strike out for the open road.

This house is not my home;
this house is simply where I have chosen
to live out the long comfort of my exile,
the body growing slow and fat in England
while the mind roams the dark forests of Poland
and the heart patrols the ruins of Jerusalem.

Who but a fool invests his trust in houses?
Imagine brick and mortar protecting anyone
when the first stones are thrown!
Who but a fool would dare to set down roots
when any pesticide can deal with wandering jew?
Why even the nails on which we hang our hats
may one day turn and call us crucifier.

No, it is never our land that we inhabit;
for land cannot be owned
except in the eyes of other men -
and in our case not even there.
Why even the Promised Land is only ours by covenant -
and that not with God but with the United Nations.

Chased out of Eden by an angry proprietor,
with no time to pack our bags
(and nothing to pack anyway
since we were supposed to go naked),
the roads have always been our exile
and our sanctuary.

I look at all the fine houses in every town I visit
and I am staggered by their complacency.
What kind of naive optimism invests in a mezuzah?

Brick and mortar will protect no one
when the first stones are thrown;
no anti-Semite will be held back
by an icon on a doorpost,
the evil eye of Yahweh
hung above a bell.
The concrete tents we put up to protect ourselves
are an unprimed canvas
waiting for the insignia of our enemies.

I am he who roams the desert and deserted streets:
Odysseus of the hooked nose,
Jason of the shrugged shoulder,
Don Quixote of the horned temple,
Bleistein with a fat cigar -
eternal Bedou of the city's sewer.

All roads lead to exile or to Israel.
I wear my hat at all times,
my shoes have no laces.
Blessed Art Thou O Lord Our God
Who Teaches Us When To Begin Walking.

Preface to Japanese Poems (1989)

Japanese poetry, that most ancient craft, is often a matter of form and technique more than of those qualities attributed to European poetry - the capturing of awe-inspiring ephemera, the glimpsing of the chimera of love, the expression of false ideas or exaggerated emotions. Not that the Japanese lack any of these, but it is the formalities which are their most obvious characteristic; just as any schoolchild beyond the age of sixteen can recognise a sonnet by its scansion and its regular construction. The choka and sedoka, the haiku and the imayo, the tenka and the dodoitsu, are rigid forms, and not easily reconstituted in the English, as much as anything because the vagaries of language are so different. English is even more compact with multivalences than the Japanese, but the manner of the ambiguities does not so straightforwardly encourage the sort of courtesies and subtleties that can be found, say, in the Pillow Book of Sei Shōnagon, or in Kokashu's marvellous lyric, collected in the Manyoshu:

Tama-dare no	Through the chinks
Osu no sukeki ni	Of the jewelled blinds
Iri-kayoi ko ne	Come to me.
Tarachine no	Should my mother ask -
Haha ga towasaba	Mother of the sagging breasts -
Kaze to mosamu	I shall say it was the wind

I make no claim to expertise in this subject. I have read anthologies - mostly in translation; sometimes with parallel texts rendered in phonetics - and I have eaten sushi, which gave me the same false feeling of having visited both Tokyo and its mirror-sister, Kyoto. Both of these were immensely pleasurable experiences, more easily repeated in my case by imitating the senryu than by trying to cook the seaweed; and anyway, like all artists, I affirm the right to recycle whatever seems worth recycling, to breathe whatever oxygen the Muse dispenses to this narrow realm of anagrams we call poetry.

Elongated Haiku Of Desire

Desire is constant and insatiable
We eat only to sustain our bodies
for the next meal
And in making love
we are already dreaming
of the next woman

There is no such thing in Japanese tradition as an "elongated Haiku"; the form is my invention. What possible grounds there could be, what possible right, for a European Jew to add a new form to the traditions of Japanese poetry, is a subject you are free to discuss among yourselves.

Song At My Birthplace

Beyond the green hills
are the stone walls of Lo-on
a city which has grown so
cosmopolitan
that even the foreigners
are today indigenous

There are no kings here
no emperors or princes
no outcasts or scavengers
The poorest flourish
the outlander is welcome
all buy in the same market

Do you hesitate
here at the crossroads looking
for the city's real name
I shall not name it
I would not wish to make it
sound any less attractive

Cento in Preparation for Yom Kippur

Why should the aged eagle stretch its wings,
the waters of Shiloh overflow their banks?
Who will be your advocate,
father of these testaments,
lord of these rain-washed firmaments,
chronicler of men?

Your old laws cling like tape-worms
to the branches of my bones.
(If I could assume prayer as part of speech)
The occasional light from your liturgy
only encourages insects.
(If I could set my flowers dancing in the rocks)

My name is Seth and I am drowning
My name is Lot and I am petrified
My name is Augustine and I am burning
My name is Argaman and I am weeping
My name is Estragon and I am waiting
My name is Mordechai and I am blameless
My name is Mersault and I have nothing to repent
My name is Marcellus and I see three dead men

Slowly the voices shaken from the yew-tree
drift away beneath the hummock of uncatalogued sand
Slowly the axe falls upon a head already severed

The aged eagle and the voices shaken from the yew-tree belong to
T.S. Eliot's "Ash Wednesday"; Eliot practised the technique of
building poems in cento, using multiple quotations from the works of
other people, so he can have no complaint when others use him the
same. The hummock of uncatalogued sand belongs to Ezra Pound,
from his "Homage to Sextus Propertius", and like the Eliot is used
both for its poetic relevance here and for the fact that both were
publicly anti-Semitic, as one might suspect God of being, given the
nature of his laws and covenant, the history he has permitted for his
chosen people these past three and a half thousand years. A poem
about Yom Kippur is of necessity a poem about passing judgements.
I leave you to uncover the other sources of these lines for yourself.

Note In My Diary, Botswana, 1978

Our father sleeps with the earth
his genitals bound with cord
her breast in the crook of his palm

Yet even these empty eggs have suppurated
They crack like walls of mud
groaning beneath this yoke of sun

At the time of writing I had no idea that this was a poem, nor that it reflected a classical Japanese technique (and is, in fact, an almost perfect exemplar of that extremely difficult technique, one indeed that may serve as a model for the use of that technique, in English, for future generations). Some lines came to me; I wrote them down; I had no idea what else to do with them; I abandoned them. Years later, studying Japanese poetry with a Japanese poet of some acclaim, I discovered that they constituted the perfection of a form.

I believe that the above statement may be an original and important contribution to the profession of literary criticism, but it will require the practice of literary criticism to explain why. That essay should be entitled: "How Poetry Gets Written".

Tenka
Florence 1981

I watch your high heels
damp-browed on the Spanish Stair
until the darkness
beyond the river cleans out
my eyes like a stone rubbed smooth

Theseus

I dwell among scorpions and spiders
To sail my boat
  the men have hoisted fishing nets onto the mast
Where others triumph with flying colours
  me - I err in black

Crematorium

Everything in this world
Has a purpose
Has a hunger
Has a need

And me?
My purpose
My hunger
My need?

Bring me fuel
More fuel
I am burning

Song Of The Intellectual In Her Boudoir

As with my clothing
so also with these dull thoughts
I am tired each day
of wearing the same gladrags
I shall purchase a new wardrobe

Several poems presented on the same page should not be misconstrued as an inference that they are in any way connected. I am simply conscious of the aesthetics, and the greenness, of space.

Song Of The Goat-Boy To His Master's Daughter

The morning was of Chinese jade
when I found your shadow resting
under the sweating yellow fronds
of a broken jacaranda

I do not know the names of God
nor have I seen the angels wrestling
only the crickets' morning-song
and the shallows of these valleys

Nor can I bring you hyacinths
for your sunlight-crested windows
touching the ciphers of your name
it is not my place to question

Yet the morning was of Chinese jade
when I found your shadow resting
under the sweating yellow fronds
of a broken jacaranda

The last poem is full of errors and problems, but no less full of love for having them.

A Japanese poet would not make reference to Chinese jade, except at certain periods of history, when Japan regarded itself as so far superior to China that it could comfortably, even condescendingly, make the claim; if this were a translation from a genuine Japanese poem, discovered by archaeologists, the reference would help us to date it.

Jacaranda do not have fronds, they have branches. Fronds do not sweat.

A Japanese goat-boy would not use the European term "God". The lady, being noble, was likely a Buddhist; the goat-boy most likely a follower of Shinto, a polytheistic cult whose names are merely names in Japanese, but in English constitute another gorgeous poem in themselves: Amaterasu-Ō-Mi-Kami , Great Spirit Who Shines in the Heavens, Ame-no-Uzume, The Great Persuader and The Heavenly Alarming Female, Fūjin, god of the wind, Inari, goddess of rice and fertility; so many more.

There are no angels in Shinto.

On reflection, an uneducated and illiterate goat-boy would have known none of the above, and could therefore have written the poem; except that, being an uneducated and illiterate goat-boy, he still could not.

All that remains, I suspect, is the need to express desire.

Song at Treblinka

What price this flesh the butcher cried
and laid his head upon a block of skulls
What price these bones
What price this dust
What price my cleaver
blunted to docility

In the hands of the executioner
Law is an axe
In the hands of the slave
Law is vengeance
In the hands of the righteous
Law is justice
In the hands of the butcher
Law is power

And on this block of skulls a head falls
echoing dull and hollow as a cleaver
The time is fast approaching
cries the butcher
when we shall have to call on innocence
to justify itself

I have a vague notion, which of course I could check if I weren't lazy, that the closing couplet belongs either to Albert Camus, or to Arthur Miller, or probably to both of them. Certainly Miller, in "After The Fall" spoke about innocence in the context of "this mountain of skulls", and Camus, in "L'Homme Revolté", made reference to slave camps under the flag of freedom, massacres justified by philanthropy, and a taste for the superhuman which tends to cripple judgment. It seems to me the fundamental dilemma of humane societies, that we wish to apply our values in every context, but in doing so we implicitly collaborate with those who do not, and are therefore in part responsible for their misdemeanours. Do we give democratic rights to someone dedicated to the overthrow of democracy? Do we allow a traumatic childhood-in-poverty to vindicate the drug-dealer, the child-abuser, and give him a humane sentence, so he can re-offend when he gets out, rather than make him forfeit his life? Do we criticise ourselves for bombing Dresden and Nagasaki into submission, when both acts saved hundreds of thousands of lives? Yes, we do.

Walking In The Country

Walking in the country
wild flowers seek me
roe deer seek me
leaves and trees seek me
lambs and calves seek me
The fools
they think there is no beauty
without poetry

This, on the other hand, unquestionably had its source in
the poetry of Bertolt Brecht, which will surprise you; you
know the name as one of the great modern dramatists, and
perhaps were unaware that he wrote songs and poems too.
His political poems are amongst the finest in the genre.

The Meeting

No meeting ever engendered more nostalgia
the person he was now
watching in memory
the person he was then
imagining his self-to-be

They met at the conjunction of two roads
the one the boulevard of dream
the other the cul-de-sac of memory
two of them coming from opposite directions
yet leaving just one set of tracks

There Are No More Gods

There are no more gods
not because we murdered them
not because they died
not even because the One God
will not tolerate rivals

The rain has lashed them
to the backs of bleeding men
The wind has woven
a winding-sheet to wrap them
in the skins of bleeding men

And sun has burned them
drier than thirst and weaker
harder than toil
or the callused skin on the
palms of a labourer's hands

Humble you told us
humble in the face of fate
humble before you
And after you? - Humility
spitting in the face of fate

Those rocks that we laid -
now you shall lie under them
Those stones that we moved -
out of the pile of rubble
shall rise up a monument

There are no more gods
no longer the cry of fate
I am the One Cry
I am the whisper of fate
Mine are the faces of God

The form of the poem is an "Imayo", which is a compound form of the Tenka; a single Tenka requires 5-7-5-7-7 syllables and has just one stanza; multiply the stanzas and it becomes an Imayo.

Song Of The Stranger
A Song Of Pesach

I walk along rugged roads
  and sleep beside still waters
    no destiny detains me
      nor any destinations

I pay no heed to signposts
  I own no love of houses
    I stand inside your doorway
      and am your excuse to eat

The idea behind this is one of the loveliest in the Jewish tradition, but perhaps also one of its most misguided. At Passover, during the ceremonial meal at home, a seat is left vacant for the prophet Elijah, the door open for him to enter, and a special glass of wine set at his place. Elijah never comes of course, but welcoming guests to the table compensates, and any Jewish traveller knows that he can find a place, because his presence validates the tradition and thereby grants permission to the host to perform the ceremony. Why is this misguided? Not because Elijah never comes – he does, in the disguise of the guest. No, it is misguided because it includes a symbolic glass of wine, and Elijah was a lifetime Nazirite. No invited guest will ever be so discourteous as to decline an offered glass of wine; how then, can any host place him in such a position of embarrassment?

The Insomniac's Meditation

Close your eyes
until the darkness rushes in
like tepid water

Slowly the mind liquefies
consciousness erodes
thought plunges
through the knotted membrane
into the pool of darkness
where sleep lives

Fanshen

Ah, they cried, the countryside,
the lovely, lovely countryside.
The fields we ploughed,
tethered to the ox's back:
the hay we gathered,
hands blistered by the hoes;
the streams we fished,
bound to the reeling line.

Ah, they cried, the countryside,
the lovely, lovely countryside.
You can smell it in the stables.
You can smell it in the paddocks.
You can smell it in the manor house.
The countryside, the countryside,
the lovely, lovely smell of progress.

In a sense this too owes a debt to Bertolt Brecht, in that David Hare's play "Fanshen", in which I played several roles in Lancaster in 1981, leaned heavily for its dramatic techniques on those of Brecht: the breakdown of the "fourth wall" especially, with actors playing multiple roles, but changing costume at the side of the circular stage, so the audience was always aware that these were actors. "Fanshen" the play, based on a book of the same name by the American Marxist William Hinton, tells of the anti-feudal revolution that took place in China when Mao came to power in 1945, a liberation on the one hand, a different kind of enslavement on the other. The process of Fanshen was similar to the "Truth and Reconciliation" of post-apartheid South Africa, except for the spirit of coercion and witch-huntery that prevailed, much as they did in Salem, Massachusetts when Abigail Williams turned her attentions upon John Proctor.

But how, an astute reader may well ask, does the Chinese concept of Fanshen find its way into a Japanese poem? A reasonable question. But also an unreasonable one. Is Flaubert to be criticised for quoting the ancient Greeks? Is Tolstoy at fault for borrowing from the French? Does it matter that Chaucer stole his tales from Boccaccio and Shakespeare his from Cinthio and Holinshed? Take away the title, and this poem goes where "Rondavel" went previously, viewing the same scene from two perspectives simultaneously: the romantic view of the countryside as seen by we who dwell in cities and yearn for the poetic fallacy of the rural idyll; the rather less fallacious view of the rural peasant, for whom cattle are work and fields require ploughing.

Preface to Coins (1993)

For several years, at the end of the 1980s and in the early 1990s, the Muse appeared to have abandoned me, or at least to have made the decision that I could serve as her amanuensis more usefully in prose than verse. Besides the "Early" the "Hebrew" and the "Japanese" poems, I had completed two other works of poetry, "Khaki On Both Sides", which were Bernhard Aaronsohn's poems in my novel "The Flaming Sword", and "The Hourglass", which is the final volume of "The Argaman Quintet". Perhaps the Muse was right. Certainly, through those several years, nothing emerged that in any way resembled poetry of an order I would wish to keep.

Then, in 1992, I found what I had been looking for in vain for several years - a translation of Rainer Maria Rilke which retained his poetic forms as well as his language and his tone and his ideas. My German simply wasn't good enough to read him meaningfully in the original, and every version I had ever read abandoned one dimension in order to ensure the others. As so often in my writing life, a great read inspired me to write, and in the space of just a few months I wrote the twenty or so poems which made up the collection I entitled "Coins".

In its proper usage, tribute is a sum of money paid in acknowledgement of subordinance, or as a mark of respect, usually but not always to a monarch or a vassal lord. One pays tribute by handing over a coin – tipping is a form of this, as are wads of notes in brown envelopes. While those rendered to God may not do so, because of the commandment against graven images, those rendered to Caesar contain an implicit irony, because the coins rendered in tribute will have the face of Caesar engraved on at least one face. With these poems, I have attempted to engrave both sides.

The cover of the original book was also a coin – a tribute to the Norwegian artist Edvard Munch; but the cover was my painting of his painting "The Scream", not the original; I found his tones too dark, his cry too searing, and christened my version "Softening The Cry". Before the holocaust, perhaps; but after it! It needed softening.

The Annunciation
(after Rainer Maria Rilke)

And so it came to pass one eveningtide
after I had awoken from my rest,
that I was sent, and walked upon the roof
of the king's house, and from the roof espied
the woman wash herself; and she, undressed,
was beautiful to look upon, in truth
more beautiful than any angel born
of Man or God, a flower in the dawn
was she, both opening and ripening,
as if a virgin - though long married -
in whom I would have gladly sewn the seed.
But I, a lesser angel - oh, indeed -
lost in awe of beauty long I tarried,
and quite forgot what I was sent to bring.

This was Rilke's conceit, not mine; but so splendid it was irresistible
to use it for a poem of my own.

Song Of The Rebel
(for Thomas More)

Upon what holy mountain did you stand,
cut by the moon's slim blade, taking refuge
in silence of inspiration, silence
of love's oblivion, silence of God's language?

Upon what sunlit terrace did you walk,
clutching the lyric rose, seeking shelter
in truth's beauty, in truth's absolution,
in truth's image on a tarnished altar?

Upon what high scaffold will you hang,
mocked by the seagulls' cackle, laughed at by
cynic doves, clutching your crown of thorns and
praying, pleading, now stoically to die?

To My Teacher
(for HJ)

As a child I tried to walk
where my teacher had walked
I followed in his footsteps
learning everything he taught

As a boy I longed to fly
where my teacher had flown
But he called me trespasser
having made the skies his own

As a youth I stole my teacher's voice
and studied how to teach
Then he taught me to go further
towards lessons beyond speech

Now the fields have all been trodden
and the skies have all been flown
What can I teach you teacher
now that I am fully grown?

I have wrestled for a long time over whether or not to spell out in full the name of the teacher who is the dedicatee of this poem; and in the end have decided not to. The poem could have been written by any student for any teacher, and to name this one would be to reduce a universalism to a unique particular, which would diminish the conceit. Plus, how much more fun to leave those who might be interested guessing!

Love Song
(after Robert Lowell)

The branches of a gnarled and withered tree
lean over the rushing brook, like some old
hermit stooping on his cane, his fingers, or its leaves,
parched by the burning sun, dipped

in the stream, made cold as frost by icy
water, thus gradually revive, unfold,
and are refreshed. So, also, love lingers
where mouth is dipped in mouth and kisses sipped

as slow as icy water from a spring.
So I, dipped in your flesh,
renew myself, and love courses in the
blood, and the brook flows onward to the sea.

After Robert Lowell, rather than for him. I had been reading my
way through his collected poems and was intrigued by the way he
had developed traditional forms into something closer to blank
verse, especially though by no means exclusively the sonnet.

Tiresias

(for and after J.L. Borges)

From the ramparts of this walled city -
higher much higher
than the ziggurat of Babel -
the eye of the blind watchman
traverses the horizon

Endless is the great sea stretching westwards
endless the bleak desert to the east
endless the dark sky

In his right hand the jewelled sword
given him by his beloved
In his left hand the book of riddles
given him by the sage

In the hours between darkness and darkness
the eye of the blind watchman
peers into oblivion
from the ramparts of a city
at the centre and circumference of the universe

And the eye turns inwards
peering now beneath the skull
behind the walls of flesh
whether upon Man
or God
or nothingness

Epitaph for W. B.

Seeking a suitable epitaph for W. B. –
in Yates' wine bar down on Regent Street;
not right, but how could I not write
something, at least, even if dyslectically –
"Those masterful images because complete
Grew in pure mind, but out of what began" might
seem like a good starting-point, if trite,
and undermined by the sequent "A mound
of refuse or the sweepings of the street."
In Yeats, throughout, masterful images abound,
rendering choice a question of what not to choose.
"An Acre Of Grass" for starters, given his mere six by three.
"Before The World Was Made", now his is after
(and no one ever accused W. B of disseminating laughter).
"Easter 1914", "Wild Swans", "Innisfree",
these are now so many clichés they can only be refused.
Then what, after Auden? "What shall I do
with this absurdity – O heart, O troubled heart?"
What can I do but raise a glass, or two,
and wonder what if anything his poetry can mend,
and watch the young in one another's arms, and send
my thoughts to him, at daybreak and a candle-end.

On Drawing
(for Henri Cartier-Bresson)

Drawing is observing. It is useless
to invent. This is no mere artefact
moulded on a potter's wheel, or carved on
marble; this is the making of a tie
(for eye and hand are indivisible)
in which the act of drawing concentrates
the inner eye intensely as the act
of prayer concentrates the soul upon
the soul of God. A drawing is not less
than an entire universe, where eye
and hand, not imagination, create
the invisible with the visible.

He was, of course, one of the great photographers of his day, the
man who invented photo-journalism, but he was also an outstanding
draughtsman. "Photography," he once said, "is an immediate reaction,
drawing is a meditation."

Psalm
(after John Donne)

Happy is the man who sleeps beside your
beauty, whose flesh is touched and quickened by
your touching flesh, whose breath, as dry and sour
as lime, is sweetened by your breath, who finds
your kiss such joy. Bodies embrace bodies,
and in the dark there is no ugliness,
no beauty; flesh is a mask, a promise
only love can fill or unfulfil. Press
then your lips, your flesh on mine, enfold me
in your darkest being; I would not mind
if you were old and ugly as a she-
wolf. The act is beautiful, the rest all
mind, and minds can sully anything. Fall
asleep beside me love. Happy am I.

Nine Character Sketches

The idea behind these character sketches came from a book by W.G. "Max" Sebald, published after his death, in which he used the ostensible form of blank verse to write what were really prose accounts of two fascinating men, the painter Matthaeus Grünewald and the botanist Georg Wilhelm Steller, the latter of whose voyage into Alaska and the Arctic with Vitus Bering had already occupied my interest in the writing of "A Journey In Time". Why should poetry not also be biography?

1. The Degradation
(for Alfred Dreyfus)

Friday January 4th should have seen
the public degradation of Alfred Dreyfus
but the courts postponed it by a day
when they realised how much more amusing it would be
if it took place on the Sabbath

Framed and condemned as a Prussian spy
the former Captain was to be deported to Devil's Island
but only after he had undergone the public humiliation
of an "execution procession"

Inmate number 164 was woken at 7.30am
his epaulettes his brass his buttons his gold officer's braid
were loosened so that they would tear more easily
his sword was scored to be sure that it would be break

Then he was searched handcuffed
delivered to the Republican Guard
Mounted troops escorted a black wagon
drawn by four horses
to the Ecole Militaire
where an iron gate was kept closed
to prevent the vast crowd spilling onto the Cour Morland

Every regiment of the Paris garrison

had sent two detachments to the ceremony
one of soldiers in arms the other of young recruits

Stiff and stoical
maintaining the steel bearing of a soldier
Dreyfus listened to the reading of the act of judgement

General Darras then stood up on his stirrups
raised his sword and declared
"Alfred Dreyfus you are not worthy of bearing arms
In the name of the French people we degrade you"
In riposte Dreyfus shouted back
"Soldiers they are degrading an innocent man
Long live France! Long live the Army!"

To which the crowd beyond the gates retorted
with cries of "Death!"

A Sergeant-Major slashed the gold braids
from his cap and uniform
stripped the regimental numbers from his collar
ripped off the brass buttons
then knelt to tear from Dreyfus' left leg
the red stripes that denoted him a soldier

Finally he broke the prisoner's sword over his knee
pulled off his scabbard and belt
and threw them to the ground

Once more Dreyfus protested his innocence

The year in question was 1895

Because it was the Sabbath
Dreyfus' family were unable
to attend the ceremony

Among those Jews who did attend were
famously
the journalist Theodor Herzl and
less famously though much more famous
the actress Sarah Bernhardt

2. In Praise Of Tightrope Walkers
(for Charles Blondin)

Charles Blondin
I sing to you on your birthday
a song of praise
knowing full well that no one else
has even heard of you
Blondin? Blondin?
Isn't he a pop star, a footballer?
Wasn't he that fascist who?
No, just a moment, I saw him in that film.
Then he must have been a friend of Byron's?
A Symbolist poet? A politician?

The truth is
he was none
but he was also all of these
for all of these walk tightropes
one way or the other
His real name was Jean-Francois Gravelet
though he styled himself Charles Blondin
and he was first presented to the public
aged five in Saint-Omer
as "The Little Wonder"

And what a wonder!
Circus tightropes anyone can do
with a little bit of training
a harness and a safety net
even the unharnessed headstands and the somersaults
that were his speciality

But Niagara Falls
on a rope stretched 160 feet above the surging water!
Blindfolded!
With a sack over his head!
Trundling a wheelbarrow!
With a man on his back!
On stilts!

One time, he got so carried away
by the need to entertain the thousands
who turned out to watch him crossing
that he stopped half-way
set up a portable grill
cooked and ate an omelette
then had a marksman with a shotgun
in a tugboat down below
fire a bull's-eye through the hat
that he was wearing

Where are you now
heirs and followers of Blondin
little wonders of the high tightrope?
Where are the artist Blondins
the politician Blondins
the scientist Blondins
where are you when we need you?
Have you all retired as he did
to that park in Ealing
where the streams are forded
by neat bridges made of planks
precisely wide enough for wheelchairs
where the nearest thing to a tightrope
is on pulleys in the kiddies' playground
supervised by trained child-minders
dug in with cement to health and safety guidelines,
and three-foot pile rugs to catch a fall
from what is anyway just six feet?

3. Chateaubriand and Mandela

"Il faut cultiver notre jardin" - Voltaire

The Vîcomte de Châteaubriand began his life-writing in 1807
at the summer house in the wooded hillsides
of the Vallée aux Loups near Aulnay
which he bought upon his return from Jerusalem

At exactly the same time he undertook to learn
the complementary craft of tree-husbandry
and recorded the progress of the saplings in his notebook

"Now they are still so small that I provide them with shade
whenever I step between them and the sun
But one day when they have grown
they will give shade to me
and look after me in my old age
as I looked after them in their youth"

Curiously Nelson Mandela says almost the same thing
in his life-writing "A Long Walk To Freedom"
speaking of the tiny space he fought for
as a garden while on Robben Island
a scrap of dusty courtyard in which
when he was not in isolation
or subject to the removal of all privileges
he was able to plant a dusty scrub
and hope the rain would water it
Eventually it did

"I feel a bond unites me with these trees"
Châteaubriand continues,
though it might as well have been Mandela
"I write sonnets elegies and odes to them
they are like children I know them all by name
and my only desire is that I should end my days among them"
And he did

So too did Mandela
though not on Robben Island

In a delightful gesture, sponsored by the BBC,
a tiny garden was constructed in the back
of Mandela's post-Presidential home in Umtata
complete with local art and artisanry,
and his mother's grinding-stone transformed into sculptury

It came as rather a surprise when he was brought to see it
I imagine Châteaubriand would have wept.

I am sure both Chateaubriand and Mandela were familiar with
Voltaire's famous remark that "Il faut cultiver notre jardin", but did
they also know Thomas More's remark, that ""The many great gardens
of the world, of literature and poetry, of painting and music, of religion
and architecture, all make the point as clear as possible: The soul
cannot thrive in the absence of a garden. If you do not want paradise,
you are not human; and if you are not human, you do not have a
soul"?

Or there is Tolkien, in "Lord of the Rings": "For you little gardener
and lover of trees, I have only a small gift. Here is set G for Galadriel,
but it may stand for garden in your tongue. In this box there is earth
from my orchard, and such blessing as Galadriel has still to bestow is
upon it. It will not keep you on your road, nor defend you against any
peril; but if you keep it and see your home again at last, then perhaps it
may reward you. Though you should find all barren and laid waste,
there will be few gardens in Middle-earth that will bloom like your
garden, if you sprinkle this earth there. Then you may remember
Galadriel, and catch a glimpse far off of Lórien, that you have seen
only in our winter. For our spring and our summer are gone by, and
they will never be seen on earth again save in memory."

4. A Letter
(for Ferdinand Lassalle)

Geneva, 27th August 1863

I can well affirm, my dear Von Doenigges,
that I am no longer a Jew,
that I do not like the Jews,
I even detest them in general.
I see in them nothing
but the very much degenerated sons
of a great but vanished past.
During past centuries of slavery
these men have acquired characteristics of slaves
and that is why I am
most unfavourably disposed towards them.
Besides, I have no contact with them.
Among my friends,
and in society which surrounds me here,
there is scarcely a single Jew.
I spend time with men who have been made slaves
and not those who have chosen it voluntarily,
men who are prisoners of a human behemoth
and not the willing foot-servants of an imaginary deity.
I run, as you are well aware,
the General German Workers Association,
of which there are now four thousand members.
I advocate state aid, German unification,
and all forms of nationalism,
and I refute Karl Marx's condemnation of the pan-Slavist Russians
as the "archenemy of Revolution".
If I tolerate Napoleon III
it is because he too is a friend of national identity.
I demand the overthrow of Hapsburg despotism
and the total dissolution of all empires.

Now it is true that I was born a Jew,
that my father received rabbinic training,
though in fact he earned his living as a merchant.
It is also true that, as a young man,
I was leader of those Jews in Breslau
who sought vengeance for the massacres of 1840.

But I am a follower of Hegel, not Maimonides.
I receive my Responsa from Garibaldi,
not from Moses Mendelsohn.
And I shall not let it be forgotten
that I spent eight long years
representing Heine in the courts of France,
and secured a settlement for the Countess von Hatzfeldt
that earned her eternal gratitude and a stipend worth a casket.
I fought, my dear Von Doenigges,
in the Revolution of 1848,
and was arrested, twice,
and wrote "Meine Assiden-Rede" during my imprisonment;
which even you cannot deny
was one of the more impressive documents
of that quixotic but still heroic insurrection.

All this, my dear Von Doenigges,
should tell you what kind of a man it is
your daughter, my beloved Helene, yearns to marry,
to whom she has already committed herself
emotionally and intellectually,
and would now be joined in physical and spiritual union.
Nonetheless you have rejected my proposal,
something in the manner of those obloquies of Friedrich Engels,
simply on the grounds that I am Jewish.
And for this reason,
and for this reason alone,
I hereby challenge you to arrange your seconds
and to meet me,
with that bag-of-wind pretender to my lady's heart
the questionably honourable Count von Racowitza
at break of dawn,
to duel.

Ferdinand Lassalle, or Lassal when he was given the name (he changed it because he thought it sounded Jewish) was a contemporary of Wagner, and a confrère in the revolution of 1848, Wagner in Leipzig and Lassalle in Düsseldorf, the significant difference between them being that Lassalle knew he was fighting in the cause of International Socialism, where Wagner didn't really have a clue what he was fighting for; but he did love a good fight.

5. Ninety Degrees North

The name's Peary, Robert Edwin Peary,
and no you haven't heard of me,
despite the fact you should have done,
because I, not Cook, not Amundsen, not Scott,
I was the first to reach the geographical North Pole,
which used to be the last frontier of human exploration,
till scientists realised there are more than three dimensions,
such as inwards to the nucleus of the atom,
and outwards to the ice below the crust of Mars,
and upwards to the mount of knowledge,
yes and downwards too,
into the darkest depths of human calumny.
I hope they've got the guts they'll need to find those poles.

Not that you need to know,
but I was born in Cresson,
which lies 40° 58' north and 78° 58' west,
80 miles from Pittsburgh, Pennsylvania,
in 1856, but moved to Maine,
the toughest journey of my life,
where I attended Bowdoin College
(the natives pronounce it Beau-din),
where Henry Wadsworth Longfellow was a student.
I graduated as a member of Delta Kappa Epsilon fraternity –
which means, I understand, a gentleman, in Inuit -
and was commissioned as a Civil Engineer Corps Officer
in the United States Navy in October, 1881.
I married the very lovely Josephine Diebitsch Peary,
and had two children with her: Marie and Robert Junior.
I should also tell you, since I'm always honest,
that Matthew Henson and I
both fathered children on Inuit women,
mine was called Ally,
while we were on our Arctic expeditions.

We made them all together, Matt and I,
explored Greenland by dog sled in 1886 and 1891;
returned to the island three times in the 1890s;
twice attempted to cross northwest Greenland over the ice cap;

discovered Navy Cliff.
How did we do it and survive?
By studying Inuit survival techniques, that's how,
by building igloos,
dressing in furs in the native fashion,
both for heat preservation
and to get rid of the extra weight of tents and sleeping bags
when on the march.
Used Inuit hunters and dog-drivers too,
invented my Peary system
of having support teams and supply caches for Arctic travel.
Josephine came too sometimes.
Lost eight of my ten toes from frost bite.

Now people are envious sons of bitches
who never leave their front parlours
unless someone's sent a chauffeured limousine,
and like to deny you your achievements
cause they can't stand the thought that someone
struggled to achieve something worth the trouble
while they were fiddling their tax returns
and wondering who won the baseball,
so all I'll say about the Jesup Land controversy
is that we found it,
and we saw Axel Heiberg too,
long before that Norwegian Sverdrup's expedition,
and the men as give me the gold medals
from the American Geographical Society
and the Royal Geographical Society of London
stated that they honored my tenacity,
and they were damned right,
because it took tenacity to get to Jesup,
and they haven't yet invented a word for what it took
to get the farthest north there is to get,
which was north of Ellesmere Island.

Now I gotta take a moment to say thanks to George Crocker,
who put up $50,000 to acquire the Roosevelt,
and cut a way through all that ice
between Greenland and Ellesmere Island,
and attain a Farthest North world record at 87° 06';
though the deniers deny me that achievement too,

from the comfort of their stone igloos
in the frozen tundra of Yale and Washington and Harvard,
where the only degrees they know are Law degrees,
certainly not ones of longitude nor latitude
(they give no latitude at all, these academic pedants),
- so many childless bachelorhoods at the Smithsonian.

87° 06' I say it was,
and get yourself out in the ice, and starve,
and lose your toes, and prove me wrong –
I challenge you.
87° 06' and returned to 86° 30' without camping,
72 nautical miles,
83 statute miles,
between sleeps,
and not a single detour.

We got back to the Roosevelt in May,
then weeks of agonizing travel,
west along the shore of Ellesmere
where we found Cape Colgate
and sighted a previously undiscovered farther-north,
named it "Crocker Land".
People say I made the place up,
but folks at the National Geographic Society
don't give you the Hubbard Gold Medal
for something they reckon you made up.

But I came here to tell you about the north pole,
because I found it first, whatever others say.
Me and 23 men set off from New York City on the Roosevelt
under the command of Captain Robert Bartlett, July 6, 1908.
Wintered near Cape Sheridan on Ellesmere Island,
then set out for the pole on February 28, 1909.
Sent the last support party back from "Bartlett Camp"
on April 1, latitude 87° 45' north.
That left just six of us,
Matt Henson and me and four Inuit,
Ootah, Egigingwah, Seegloo and Ooqueah.
Set up "Camp Jesup" in honour of my greatest sponsor,
on April 6 it was, not five miles from the pole.
Hit the point on April 7.

90° dead.
We nearly were too, from hunger, and exhaustion.

Now, all these years later,
it's as much as I can do to make an expedition
to the liquor store on Eagle Island
and pick up a newspaper
to read all my detractors saying
I never done this and I never done that,
and Congress wanting to send an expedition to prove it,
like as if the footprints haven't blown away.
Or if not me then Freddie Cook,
who was my surgeon on the 1891 expedition,
and if he says he made it to the Pole,
then I trust his instruments
more than I trust those jealous stay-at-homes
at the Smithsonian,
and I couldn't care a monument in Greenland
whether he discovered it and I attained it,
or the other way around,
or both, or neither,
and whether you can prove it or you can't,
cause the whole point ain't the North Pole anyway,
that's just a round number you stake out in eternity
like an igloo in the ice or a triangle in spherical trigonometry.

No point telling that to Congressmen and academics though.
They'd say there isn't a north pole,
if they thought it would win them votes or research fellowships.

My toes hurt.

Robert Edwin Peary was born in Cresson, Pennsylvania, in 1856, and died in Washington D.C. on February 20th 1920. Officially the first men to reach the north pole were Aleksandr Kuznetsov's Sever-2 expedition between March and May 1948, though popular myth still grants the claim to Roald Amundsen's expedition of 1926.

6. To Be Carved On His Tombstone
(for D. H. Lawrence)

There was a pile of books on my bedroom floor,
old books, second-hand books,
picked up months before
at bargain prices from a remainder store,
the pages black with someone's garbled notes,
some failed A-level student
trying to dissect
or maybe, hopefully, to vivisect this density.

They were dead things, even when they were first created,
black tombstone fonts of words
laid out in rows like cemeteries.
Some piece of unoiled metal must have ground away for hours
in the making of them,
metal grinding over metal,
ink blocks stamping like soldiers on the road to war,
making curlicues on letters like the poppies
that grow up on soldiers' unmarked graves,
spitting out scraps of half-price paper
on which cheap ink's already blurred,
wrapped in only slightly thicker cover-paper,
still not thick enough to shield it
from the ravages of time and human hand,
someone's attempt to mine a profit
out of the carbon of human personality.
But dead.
Entirely dead.

They can't help it, of course.
They don't mean to be,
but books are dead things,
inanimate objects that you fall asleep to,
time-fillers on the unoiled metal train journeys
into the dark tunnels of personal schedules and timetables,
the vicissitudes of solitary crowded ticket queues,
the landscapes of old battlefields and torn-down crosses
above that other graveyard of the eternal book.

This particular pile of books had entirely white covers,
most of them torn or damaged,
a cartoon penguin,
a photograph of no particular relevance to the title,
the author's name,
the title of the book,
and on the back a blurb, a résumé,
a photo of the author,
just like every other book.
And I found myself thinking again:
dead words, black mortuary print.
An emptiness.

But these were not just any books.
These were the complete works,
in paperback,
of D.H. Lawrence,
every one of them from The White Peacock
through his poems essays letters stories,
through The Rainbow and Women In Love,
through Lady Chatterley and the Phoenix,
all the way to The Man Who Died
but didn't.
Twenty three volumes at 60p a time,
or take the whole lot for a tenner.

Never in the whole history of literature
has a man of such exuberance
poured so much of himself,
so much that is vital, intense and vigorous,
so much passion for the joys of life,
for the colours and the sounds and smells,
the flowers and the love affairs,
the snakes and the mountain lions,
the ancient peoples and the modern peoples,
the whole gamut of human growth
and struggle and exasperation,
poured it and poured himself
perfectly coherent
even when the consumption made him cough and splutter,
poured it like printer's ink into these white sepulchral volumes
piled pyramidically upon my bedroom floor.

And I wondered, trying to capture his voice,
what he would have made of this,
and I thought, he can't have minded,
since he give his life to making mausoleums such as these.
He must have known.
He must have understood.
That human imagination does not lie in books,
nor even in the words of books,
but in the dialogue between the writer and the reader,
the one inscribing the marble tombstone
so the other can come by
and dream
and resurrect.

And I understood in that moment that a dead book
is not different from a dead human being
standing on the football terrace
with his life lived vicariously
through someone's else glories,
or vomiting in a pub too drunk even to fantasise
a night of passion with the woman opposite,
or rummaging through the barren catacombs
of some about-to-be-shut-down bookstore
for someone else's books,
for someone else's life.

And so I picked up the first volume
and began to read,
and for the next several months continued reading
until I had relived the complete works
that I had first lived as a student of seventeen,
and at the very last I re-read Frieda's terrible biography
with its gut-wrenching account of his final days,
a dead book written about a dead man.
"Death was there", she said of him, "Lawrence was dead.
So simple, so small a change
yet so final, so staggering.
Death!"

Right there, in mortuary ink
on white sepulchral paper,
in a book shaped like a tombstone,
row upon dead row.

"There had been the change,
he belonged somewhere else now,
to all the elements;
he was the earth and sky,
but no longer a living man.
Lawrence, my Lorenzo,
who had loved me and I him...
he was dead..."

But you were wrong, Frieda, wrong, wrong, wrong.
What you were describing was not the negative
of a man descending into death.
Rather it was the heroic triumph of a demi-god,
ascending abjectly into immortality.

The Anglo-Saxon world has come, in the last few years, to reject
Lawrence, even to despise him, mostly for the same reason that it
spends so much fatuous endeavour seeking someone else who can
be held to have written Shakespeare's plays – the middle classes
cannot bear the idea that someone from the urban peasantry or the
rural working class should rise to quite such intellectual and artistic
heights. They have to be put back in their place, which is at the side
entrance, by the tradesman's door. But the simple fact is, that in the
entire annals of Anglo-Saxon creative thought, there are only two
men of true genius, and they are Shakespeare and Lawrence. The
prophet is always without honour in his native land. One day his
detractors will understand that they have something to expiate.

7. Heresies
(for Galileo Galilei)

1642
at Arcetri
near Florence
under house arrest
working only under close policing
completely blind
censured by the ecclesiastical authorities
sentenced to death by Pope Urban VIII
(commuted at the personal behest of the Duke of Tuscany)
on the 65th birthday of the Danish astronomer Johannes Fabricius
(the man who actually discovered sunspots)
on the anniversary of the death of Marco Polo
at the age of 77
Galileo Galilei
died
broken on the rack of disappointment

Of his achievements we can list:

the inference
from the oscillations of a lamp
suspended in the cathedral at Pisa
of the usefulness of a pendulum
in measuring time exactly

the invention of a hydrostatic balance
a treatise on the law of specific gravity
the theory of falling bodies
the invention of the thermometer
and the proportional compass
the development of the refracting telescope
and its use in determining
the nature of the lunar landscape
the discernment of the structure of the Milky Way
the discovery of four satellites of Jupiter
the proof of solar rotation
based on the evidence of sunspots
the law of uniformly accelerated motion

the law of the parabolic path of projectiles
the law of virtual velocities
the law of inevitable weightedness

All these
science
or heresy
depending on your point of view

The list of poems banned as heresies, whether religious, political, moral or social, is too long for this page. Noteworthy among them is Ovid's "Ars Amatoria", which upset the Roman Emperor Augustus so much that he both banned the work and banished the poet; the poem survived, until the monk Savonarola included it in his "Bonfire of the Vanities" in 1497. Christopher Marlowe translated it into English in 1599, only to find his version banned and himself imprisoned; and U.S. customs added it to their list in 1930. The 1881 edition of Walt Whitman's endlessly rewritten and reprinted canonical "Leaves of Grass" was banned in Boston, though that city now requires study of it as part of its Literature programme in secondary schools; required reading and banning are of course both forms of coercion and control. The French government suppressed six of the poems in Baudelaire's "Les Fleurs du Mal" and charged him with corrupting public morals; the work was republished the following year and has never been out-of-print since. The complete works of Osip Mandelstam disappeared on Stalin's orders, with the poet banished to death-by-exile. Alan Ginsberg's "Howl" fell victim to an obscenity trial in 1957. "Education for Leisure" by the current English Poet Laureate Carol Anne Duffy was banned in 2008 by the school's examinations board AQA...plus ça change...

8. 1 Awoke Hearing Voices Late Last Night
(for Joan and Daniel, but also for GBS)

I awoke hearing voices late last night
and thought it must be schizophrenia
but it wasn't
it was Joan of Arc
screaming through the darkness
a high-pitched wail that wasn't ecstasy
a voice impaled on its own grimacing
as eternal fire burned the flesh away

Why has it taken me, she said,
five hundred years to earn my sainthood
when that bastard G. B. Shaw
just wrote a rotten play about me
and won the Nobel Prize in sixty-nine?

It seemed an entirely reasonable lament
though not perhaps
the one I had expected

There were various other
rantings and ravings
howlings through the smoke
screeches through the agony

I heard the name Mark Twain
in one particularly infernal moment
and a neat pun about putting
Bertolt Brecht into the stockyards
with Ingrid or was it Ingmar Bergman?
She seemed to have a gripe against Shakespeare too
and some Hollywood director who she claimed
had botched her story altogether

She grumbled on and on
interminable as the flames
until it seemed posterity had treated her
far worse than Henry and his inquisition

How can you sleep with voices shouting in your head?

I turned on the light but that only encouraged her
I lit a cigarette – still worse
It felt as though her hand were reaching
for the lighted match

Dieu o grazisc e a mos huoills, she said
in what I took for mediaeval French
Que per lor conoissensam venc.
Jois, qu'adreich auci e fola
L'ira qu'ieu n'aqui e l'anta
Er va sus,
Qui qu'en mus,
D'Amor don sui fis e frems;
C'ab lieis c'al cor plus m'azauta
Sui liatz ab ferma cord.

They sounded very pained and very beautiful
these schizophrenic voices calling me to do
what sadly was fated never to be understood

The words in the penultimate stanza are from the 12th century
Provençal poet Daniel Artaud, one of the greatest of all time in any
language, and the man especially honoured by Dante, who quotes him
in Canto 26 of the Purgatorio, and not in translation into Italian, but in
his original Provençal. The version here is Ezra Pound's translation,
and reads: "I thank my God and mine eyes too,/Since through them
the perceptions reach./Porters of joys that have refuted/Every ache
and shame I've tasted;/They reduce/Pains, and noose/Me in Amor's
corded net./Her beauty in me prevaileth/Till bonds seem but joy's
advancing."

9. Photographs
(for Louis Daguerre)

The year is 1839.

Louis Daguerre is taking the first ever
photograph of the moon
and I am guessing that he chose today
because the moon was full.

To what extent is this lunology?
To what extent a cameraman's need
for something suitable to photograph?

He will need to leave the shutter open
for an immensely long time –
even a modern camera will need
up to ten minutes –
during which the appearance of circularity
at the edges of the moon's disc
will reveal its illusoriness;
but the quality of the recorded image
will re-blur it.

What will he see,
through the sophisticated eye
of so primitive an apparatus?

No shadows,
but just a medley of bright or dark markings.

Just left of centre, the moon's iris,
shining back at him;
will he know that it is named
after that other luminary, Nicholas Copernicus?

Most probably not.
He is a man of ideas and technologies,
who has invented a new machine,
and needs proof of its virtues

in order to secure financial backing
and an enthusiastic market.

The names of the grey patches mean nothing to him,
provided their image is distinct.

He has no notion that men will see this photograph,
and dream of walking on its surface.

He has no means of knowing that Jose Arcadio Buendia
will be driven mad by this infernal instrument,
believing it has the magic power
to render proof of God

He cannot conceive that one day,
more than a century and a half later,
staring at a much better lunar map
provided by the men aboard Apollo 17
I will look up from my desk
towards the full moon engravured in my window
and chart the medley of bright markings
that are this poem

To make a daguerreotype portrait you would need to polish a silver-coated copper plate with a long buffer until the surface is highly reflective, then sensitise it with chloride of iodine or bromine. Place it in the camera, ideally on a high shelf, and expose the image to the lens for a long time. Back in your darkroom, use fumes from heated mercury to bring out the image from the plate, and then fix it by bathing the plate in hyposulphate of soda before washing it in distilled water and leaving it to dry. Digital cameras are unquestionably simpler.

Five Songs For My Daughter

1. "GA"

Her first word - or first intelligible
sound - a kind of "ga", trying to say "cat",
gradually extended to include all
small and furry creatures, and after that
all creatures giving pleasure, meaning love.
Thus even parents become "ga", all toys,
all sights and sounds familiar enough
to indicate security; not boys,
but little girls, even some grown-ups - yes,
and certain favourite places. All of these,
expressed in just one simple sound and nod
and smile, accompanied by happiness,
giving to her who still lives on her knees
a universal symbol, "ga", or god.

2. Achilles, 11 Months, 1 Day

Desperate struggle! She writhes like some great
wriggling hippopotamus in the deep
muddy wallows of a river's bank. Then,
as if she were encountering the reeds
and rushes of the Nile, or the slate
boulders of the Eiger with its huge, steep
falls upon vertiginous rock; or when,
faced by the mightiest of deeds,
the hero of all heroes finds within
the strength to do as none has done before -
so she, too, writhes and struggles once again,
till lo! the child has crawled from cot to floor.

3. Your Birthright

This innocence is your birthright, this mere
unknowing, this too-soon-to-have-learned; not
ignorance, but a world which does not yet
contain knowledge of good and bad, nor fear
of Death. Naked in your twelvemonth Eden
you laugh and play, reminding us our chance
of happiness has come to fruit. Then dance
and be happy now, fulfil your season.
Soon we will let our serpents, rotten
fruits of inhumanity, war, pain, strife,
grim harvest of our human lot - all this
we'll feed you, your future unbegotten.
So we, who've wrecked our chance of innocence,
will thus conspire with guilt to spoil your life.

4. Queendom

No words, no gods, no sex, no enmities,
no wars, no crimes, no futile scurrying
about for bread in camps for refugees
or city slums - none of that life-or-death.

Still, a musical bear, a set of keys,
her parents' love (and ceaseless worrying!),
a book, a staircase climbed on padded knees,
a window moistened by her morning breath,

a rocking-horse, the dolls she loves to nurse,
the cats she is afraid to go too near,
her cot, the trunk she empties of her games -

just these - and yet in these the universe,
all dream and disappointment, hope and fear,
all love, all loss, the whole world is contained.

5. Adam

"Oh!" she cries, in wonder, fascination
and amazement. "Oh! Look! Diddy! Look! Ball!
Look - tree! Look - Diddy - house!" naming anew
the world as if in the beginning. Thus

Adam (Man's childhood, God's first Creation -
though born, it's said, aged thirty-three) gave all
God's creatures names (presumably in Hebrew)
crying: "Look, God - Dodo! Look! Platypus!"

Thus: recognising the familiar,
pointing, wondering, remembering, she
ordains for every object its true name
("Oh, Diddy, look - flower! Look - dog! Look - chair!")
till naming, checking, then repeating, she
assures herself her world remains the same.

No doubt my younger daughter will be quite upset when she discovers that I wrote five poems for her elder sister, and only one, and a comic poem at that, for her (see "The Ballad of the Sick Child" on page 178). The only meaningful response I can offer is: see "Cordelia's Lament" on page 161.

The Pulse

This is it then - logos of the human
pulse: the cards mis-shuffled, the pack mis-dealt
(shuffled and dealt by knaves to threadbare kings)
No spirit of unearthly numen,
no Icarus on sun-blenched, sea-drenched wings,'
rather a Sicilian gambit, fated
to falter stumbling into some Fool's Mate.
In the beginning was the Word, mis-spelled.

Imagine a Neolithic troglodyte,
armed with stick and tinder, crouching supine
at the cave-door, witnessing a full moon
in full eclipse. The uncreated night
yields only to bats' wings, the distant tune
of courting eagles in an eeriness
of wind, shadows of unformed shadows, twined
demoniacal shapes of superstitiousness.

So stick and tinder kindle earthly fire:
but it is nothing; less than the nothing
of primordial nothing in whose dark
systole-diastole the pulse is formed.
So eyes stare awe-struck, eyelids tense as wire.
The black corona passes, and is born
into a blazing aureole; a spark -
and God is fashioned on an eagle's wing.

So much for the primitive conception.
Ours is no less primitive, though ours is
magnified, exalted, reasoned by minds
too profound to fathom their own shallow
simpleness; empirical deceptions,
truths that are but the apotheosis
of uncertainty; all this we swallow,
needing to give credence - and remain blind.

When the black corona of ignorance
blazes into the bright aureole of
knowledge, we sleep secure. Stick and tinder
kindle earthly fire; savant shamans dance
ecstatic in the orgiastic rites
of certainty. But fire burns to cinder.
When we too are eclipsed, what light above
will grant us sleep on future uncreated nights?

"The Pulse" was the title-poem – the eponym to use language with absolute precision, as poetry should – of my sixth collection of poems. As with each of the previous, I was looking to try new approaches, new perspectives, which included using some of the very oldest, most traditional forms, which I had previously avoided. So Shakespeare became the recipient of a double-sonnet; so Kafka, that most prosaic of all writers, found himself admired in rhyming verse; so the iambic pentameter found itself in use again ("Song of Patience", "Edges"), albeit in blank verse or mixed rhyme-and-blank.. So I tried my hand at riddles and villanelles, and played around with rhyme, refusing in the end to accept the existence of blank verse, experimenting with homonyms and homophones, with off-centred rhyme and broken rhyme. Why not, after all, the tried and tested forms, if there is a way to make them new again? Form in the end is just a vehicle. Blank verse can be blank in other ways than lack-of-rhyme, if even the most accomplished poet has nothing worth the saying.

Song Of Patience

Primed, bridled, frontispieced
(yet fragmented,
undermined by doubt and a damp motor,
resuming take-off after two false starts),
the seasoned spirit in its cork-stopped gourd
rubs the lamp of mucus from its inner
eye, and summons up a human genie,
as yet unrhymed - for rhyme is the balance
that we ourselves, in time, articulate.

Then wait, in the cutting of the foetal cord,
Wait, in the stillness of the new-born hour.
Wait for the pouring out of nothingness,
and for the pouring in of nothingness.

We are not who we are. Homogenous,
our fathers make us in their likenesses,
which is to say the image of the man
they failed to be, the likeness of a plan
they left imperfect, whose incompleteness
may be finished and fulfilled through us.

Our mothers nurture us like fledgling birds,
comfort our cries, soothe us with tender words,
stretch the umbilicus to help us fly,
yet hold us back, not meaning to tether
us. But the umbilicus is never
cut, till mermaid voices beckon and we cry.

Then wait, in the cutting of the foetal cord.
Wait, in the stillness of the new-born hour.
Like a bondsman, hatched from the yoke of slavery
into the servitude of liberty,
wait for the pouring out of nothingness,
and for the pouring in of nothingness

Kafka's Worm

Though the thickness of the undergrowth impedes him,
though doubt throws obstacles across his path,
though clearings of illusory light deceive him -
still he goes on grappling through the dark,

wriggling like a bifurcated spider
trying to reconcile two contradictory halves:
the joy forever rising up inside him,
the anguish meanwhile spreading through his calves.

Left and right are equally untenable,
for rejection is implied in every act of choice,
and every act of hope implies dejection,
for the silence is the darkness given voice.

Yet he goes on struggling, jib and mainsail for'ard,
knowing he does so out of cowardice, not fortitude;
the path is his to choose, however rough and awkward,
yet he chooses not in freedom but in servitude.

The goal, of course, is halting - but he cannot halt,
not, at least, until he has attained his goal;
and the darkness presses deeper, and the vaults
of darkness close around the halter of his soul.

And the darkness masks itself as lightness to deceive him,
for his skin has turned to silk as thin as cloud,
weaving the cocoon of his own unhatched creation
he sloughs the blackened husk of his own shroud.

Soon enough the birds will come in harness
to breakfast on his liver, share by share.
It will not nourish them. Reduced to mere skein of darkness,
he has become as insubstantial as the air.

Child

Child, you are not who you are,
But like a barn-door painted thrice too oft,
Over-varnished, re-cut to fit the loft,
Then hammered, wrought,
Re-scratched, re-painted,
Till the wood is malleably soft.

Parents, peers, professors of unlearning
And unsound advice - unheed them all.
Coffin-makers of the soul,
Carpenters of conscience
Exercising strict control - all
Must be stripped away:
Layer upon layer of learned existence.

Now you must remove the nails,
Immerse your soul in acid,
Let out the sap, the grume, the cruor,
Galvanise the gonads,
Stir up the sanies,
Quicken the haemads,
Manumit the grains of being
That the human godling may be carved
Out of the scrap.

Then chisel, cut by ever-deepening cut,
Slough with the plane each new-grown skin,
Render bone naked, member nude,
Buttress the broken heart in barbicans of flesh.

He who you would be will be,
The hand-cast Golem, self-made Adam,
Self-invigorated, self-inspirited,
Born of the virgin footsteps,
Risen like a phoenix from its wounds.

Edges

The street beckons: brushing against clothes or
bones or flesh; a jostling contact that is
straightaway short-circuited; a muttered
word of greeting or apology; doors
held open; a smile or frown in stasis;
requests for food or information uttered
by faces to faces without names or
personalities; plugs without fuses,
subsumed in the swirling current, shuttered.

The window beckons: a girl in a white
dress irons her laundry; a car arrests
the silence in a screech of brakes; rain soaks
the lovers huddled in a doorway; night
confirms the loneliness which dark attests.
Sadder than a TV screen, the glass evokes
the bland mundaneness of the local news:
a whore loiters, a thief prowls, a cat mews.

The room beckons: books whose characters have
become as intimate, whose authors have
become familiar as real friends;
the music on the turntable; cat hairs;
ornaments dusted and replaced; fag-ends
of lonely evenings; clothes strewn across chairs;
the unsipped mugs of coffee, set in pairs.

The dream beckons: a word, or touch, or gesture
that might tap the current and complete it,
earthing the soul in the body's fissure,
joining the live and neutral pulses,
fusing the wires, closing the circuit.

But the contact is not made,
for these are the edges, only the edges.
What is lacking is the centre.

The Muse

She came to me in deepest darkness
unexpected - unexpected!? -
never was poet more atheist of her existence

But she came to me
illuminatress of the darkness
she grew like seeds of light upon my eyelids
washed them clean like morning dew
(these were the kinds of simile I used
before her visitation)
so beautiful - so beautiful

She came
I understood
to make me eloquent
but her presence merely numbed me speechless

"Is it really you?" I asked
the sort of asinine banality
a stammerer might speak at Horeb
or a bosun of Odysseus before the rocks
but surely not a poet-now-to-be?

"Is it? Is it really you?"
She smiled but did not speak
for she had brought speech for my lips
not her own

"Is it? Is it really you?
The same who came to Milton
and led him like a guide dog into Paradise?
The same who windlassed Dante through the Inferno?
The same who bridled Shakespeare
and rode him into Elsinore and Dunsinane?
The same who deafened Beethoven,
starved Mozart,
drove Van Gogh to madness
sent Mandelstam to Voronezh?
Is it? Is it really you?"

She smiled, nodded, shone
but spoke neither no nor yes.
Already this poem was half-written
even as I pretended she had got the wrong address

At what point may poetry permit itself the luxury, or is it the indulgence, of polemic? In many poetry circles, the act of writing is a form of psychic, emotional, spiritual therapy, a giving of outward expression to the struggles of the inner life, seeking catharsis through articulation, exactly as a patient does on the analyst's couch or the penitent in the confession-booth. Many of my own poems inhabit this circle. But what if the struggle of the inner life is not about love or parents, trees or skyscrapers, sexual craving or loss of faith in god? What if depression is the consequence of politics or solitude the result of economic crisis? The canon of European poetry tends towards Keats' delusion that "Beauty is Truth, Truth Beauty", wanting it to be so, whereas reality tends to replace Beauty with the more commonplace Ugliness, from which the poetry of war and wastelands emerged in the 20th century. Japanese preferred the courtly, as did that of the Troubadours of mediaeval France; Milton and Dante, among others, chose the allegorical route, through myth which is also called religion. But the wider circle also includes Brecht and Neruda, Garcia Lorca and Mandelstam, Yevtushenko and occasionally Yeats; always Shelley. Any more than theatre, music, dance, sculpture or the novel, it is not the "job" of poetry to focus exclusively on what is aesthetically beautiful. We have also to confront the ugliness.

After Auschwitz

"After Auschwitz," said the man on the TV,
"one simply can't conceive of lyric poetry" -
for the literal and metaphorical,
the physical and metaphysical,
all opposites, antitheses,
all antonyms on earth and seas,
all arguments and paradoxes under heaven
have been baked in ovens without yeast or leaven,
at a temperature of pure Davidian degrees;
then iced with radiance of Zyklon-B,
and seared, vulcanised, the somethingness made none,
till there is nothing, new or ancient,
agreeable or disagreeable,
left under the sun.

Among the ashes, literally as well
as metaphorically, the sunflowers grow.
Visitors complain about the smell -
the lines of visitors who move as slow
as chosen people marching to the showers,
their heads bent down exactly like sunflowers.
The smell is bone meal, compost and manure,
some natural dung unnaturally pure,
decomposing row by unmarked row
among the ashes of the northern bowers.

Sunlight over Auschwitz is no less beautiful
than sunlight over Chamonix or Biarritz,
nor are the gardens any less colourful
than Monet's in Giverny, or the blitz-
krieged beds at Kew. Tourists seeking a brief
respite from the chamber of horrors which is
History have been known to stroll here, leaf
to leaf and hand in hand; and Catholic nuns,
whether in black smock or coloured britches,
kneel in idolatrous worship of the sons
of God, the ones who outlived dead Jehovah,
and reinvigorate the ancient rites
by fertilising lifeless soil, turning over

the marriage-bed of earth, till sunlight
has penetrated and overpowered night.

In sleep your body lies as still
as that child I once saw in a film
about the camps, lying beside her mother -
as close as one would lie beside a lover -
in a carefully selected barrack bed.
She did not, I presume, survive. And yet
there is no guilt, no sense of sin
in me, no hesitating to recall the dead;
I am not one who says forgive-forget.
Merely I touch your thighs, your breasts, within
the deep embrace of flesh on flesh. I feel
again the shudder of that movie reel
and close my eyes to make the film expire.
Your legs wrap round me like a blanket of barbed wire.

Sweet Yehudit, let us inhabit each
other's body once again; let us make
a melodrama of our brief affair
(I nearly said "soap-opera" - ah, words! Beware!)
Let us whisper schmaltzy pillow-talk, teach
ourselves the sentimental way; let us wake
up very late, and maybe pray the morning
service quickly, then drive to Warsaw. So we
shall tell the others how we heard the warning,
how we alone survived, escaped the strife,
understood that what must be must be -
and got on with the tedious banalities of life.

For wherefore did they die? For eternal
mourning? For a thousand year vigil? For
each of us to put on black, infernal
sackcloth, to bow our heads like Auschwitz Jews,
to offer up in sacrifice still more
unconsummated hearts and souls and lives?
No, Yehudit, this is the night of the long knives,
on which we sever with our bodies all the knots of History,
honouring the past, sailing the Vistula
towards as-yet-unborn posterity.
Here on this mound of skulls I give you kisses.

Here on this flowery grave make good your wishes.

"After Auschwitz," said the man on the TV,
"one simply can't conceive of lyric poetry."
The Romans said much the same after Caligula,
and the Egyptians likewise after the Red Sea.

Ah, the great debate over whether or not poetry should rhyme.
Because it's easier to remember if you have trigger rhyme-words.
Because it was once the convention. Because poetry in its primitive
form was sung, and songs work better when they rhyme. Because
making things rhyme is equivalent to making things harmonious,
establishing the illusion of order where previously there was only the
illusion of disorder. If I have chosen to use the technique on this
occasion, it is partly as a retort to the ludicrous suggestion that lyric
poetry is barbaric after the Holocaust, partly, in the spirit of my fourth
"because", as a way of trying to make History rhyme.

Sonnet

Donne or Shakespeare might well have noted how
the branches of this gnarled and withered tree
lean over the rushing brook like some old
hermit stooping on his cane; have written

(fresh then, if now cliché) how his fingers,
or its leaves, parched by the burning sun,
dipped in the stream, frosted cold by icy
water, thus gradually revive, unfold,

and are refreshed. A fine conceit. But now
merely conceited even to attempt
to revive the freshness of a gnarled and
withered form. Forget trees, and rhymes. I shall

dip my flesh in your flesh, renew myself,
and leave the book of sonnets on the shelf.

The Prophets Of Loss

You trade in gloom, you prophets of loss,
swimmers in cold seas, inhabitants of greyness.
You drink from a half-empty glass
and lose the one-horse race
mistaking infinite variety for endless sameness.

There where the stone bleeds
and faith cracks its skull
against an empty sky,
those who can should clutch the breeze
till hope ripens.

A Song In Welsh

By nativity an Englishman - though far from native -
born among "cor blimeys", schooled in genitives and datives
by aged paedophiles in gowns of greenish mould,
I fielded at third man, a true child of the wold.
England was all smug scones and snobbish sandwiches, complacent
cream teas served to us outsiders in adjacent
rooms adorned by statues of Disraeli and a King James Bible.
Shakespeare on Saturdays, chapel on Yom Kippur, a tribal
amphictyony of Houses named for English heroes of the glorious
past - a past in truth less glorious than spurious.

Englishmen inhabit England, a land that stretches east for ever,
to the never-setting sun of Vikram's corner-shop. But never
into Cornwall, Ireland or the Scottish Isles - that land is Britain,
a land of history and culture preferred untaught and left unwritten.
The English, like their German and their Russian cousins, have their
        Pales.
In Anglo-Saxon the word for "foreigner" is "Wales".

The OED defines the wold as "open or uncultivated land",
meaning the downs and moors and peaks and mendips, the bland
infertile viscera inhabited by sheep and yokels,
an English city-dwellers traffic-jam in summer, elsewise a focal
point for mockery in silly accents by those aspiring to the Greek
and Norman modes of civilised barbarity.

                    Yet what they speak
is what I speak, the tongue of the outsider, and our affinity
is rooted in a common soil, a shared divinity -
not God, but Hatedness, expressed contemptuously through
stiffened lips that mutter hypocritic hymns from empty pews.

So it is not strange that I, a Jew, grandchild
of the stadtl and the ghetto, inhabit now this wild
hinterland, this aboriginal viscera of the wold, this rustic fen,
and share my song of strangerhood with British men.

Act Of Faith

Concupiscence of mortal flesh,
the barbs, the weals of cupid's pence,
spent in lucid somnolence,
in nonchalance, in penitence,
till all lust is forgotten...

And in time all will be forgotten,
all time, all lust, the gods themselves forgotten,
the little cross of balsa wood
you set weeping on your shoulder,
the mountain you ascended with your boulder,
the seeds you sowed in wintry weather,
their fruit now rotten, children unbegotten,
the stone quarries emptied of their rubble,
the river-beds reduced to gorse and heather,
the corn fields stubbled.

All this will be forgotten,
each venture brought to its fruition,
each word to silence,
each structure broken,
each rhyme fragmented,
each new endeavour rendered futile
in the fact of consummation,
each human act engendered and negated
in the fading flower of its accomplishment,
light formed, nothingness transcended,
only that it may be refunded into darkest nothingness.

Once more, and yet once more,
the primordial voice pronounces its heresy of creation,
dividing its firmament,
defining its order and disorder,
harnessing its own chaos,
knowing that its end must be that very nothingness
in whose dark void the primordial voice is hatched.

So I shall go on excavating
the very mine of all futility,
quarrying darkness, rummaging in the rubble
for a block of building stone,
ploughing, furrowing,
casting my seed into the compost of creation,
praying for rain.

What matters is not the beginning,
but the beginning again.

Diaries confirm precise dates on which poems are completed, but in truth these dates are meaningless. A seed for a poem can be planted, even unconsciously, years before the act of writing, or even the act of thinking about writing, and then some thought or experience, some overheard phrase, will trigger the act of writing. And even that may not lead to the poem, but only, perhaps, to some phrase written down unfinished, to which one returns, perhaps years later, and then modifies, picking up a different seed or a different phrase, experienced or written down elsewhere. So the trial of Shakespeare's father on charges of usury may have seeded The Merchant of Venice, and seeing Marlow's "The Rich Jew of Malta" triggered the writing of the play, while his employment by the Earl of Leicester furnished him with Antonio and gossip about the Queen the Portia scenes. Seeds which grow, then hybrid, then germinate together. And then, reading the finished work, something one had not considered about the poem plants a new seed, which leads to a rewriting, or a new poem. Endlessly, the beginning, and the beginning again.

A Riddle

My first is the antelope ox
My second is two houses
My third is three camels
My fourth is four doors

My fifth is the lattices of five windows
My sixth six hooks and nails
My seventh is a weapon, seven spears
My eighth two squares of fence and hedge
My ninth is the serpent of the ninefold goddess
My tenth the ten fingers that make a hand

My next is a palm, or the wings of a bird, twentyfold
My next an ox-goad, wielded thirtyfold
My next the water, full forty waves
My next enough fish for a quinquereme
My next a prop to sustain two full months
My next the eye of the septuagint
My next speaks the number of eighty mouths
My next wields the handles of ninety scythes
My next is the hole in the hundredfold axe
My next is the source of two hundred heads

Then three hundred teeth leave three hundred marks
And four hundred crosses are the branding of an ass

This belongs to my novel "City of Peace", where I invented it for King David. A slight knowledge of Hebrew will help resolve it, though knowledge of Greek should be sufficient.

In Cheddar Gorge

In Cheddar Gorge
   the grey rocks
      the granite rocks
the filaments of flung rocks
the deep fissures
         in the cleft rocks
and the rooks' nests
         in the cliff face
and the fossils forged
         in the chill air
where man rocks
   at the slow pace
      and the dizzy grace
         of cold prayer

The sheer gorgeousness of the sheer gorge
   extends from the high crags
      to the deep coombes
from the siren outcrops of meteoric rock
   to the cut shards of volcanic rock
Cold caves dug beneath the live rocks
   their icicles a cryptic code
      engraved upon the tomb rocks
         the hieroglyphs of some poor devil's lair
and in the lofty air
at every manageable and unimaginable angle
   granite grey or grass green
      ivy-clad or strung with ferns
the overhanging limbs of ancient trees
   dangle perpendicular against the falling screes

The steps of rocks ingress upon the pillars
of a natural temple
      altared by dolmens
(altered primordially by a tantrum of the gods -
the smashing of tectonic plates
   against the walls of rocks)
obelisks of original rock
   pyramids of natural rock

111

catacombs of raw crude rock
  tumuli cut in the cathedral rock
in pulse of tree and pulse of rock
  monolith and tabernacle
      shrine and nave -
        pure rock

The human voice requires a song
  to sing the god and gorge within
and harmonise it with the silence
  of the gods without
to echo pulse of tree and pulse of rock
  in the beating rhythm of the human heart
and transform godly silence
  into human shout

Any liturgy will do -
      psalm or veda
        ode or hymn
Words are irrelevant in the end
  whatever their significance in the beginning
Only their rising upwards through the human gorge
  to issue
      carved in stone
           not rock
reduced to cairn or cottage
        wall or track
and the presumption of the humanly superior
  in a pitted road
      an empty church
        a dug quarry -
and the rock
  the rock forever at our back

Worship the hanging tree
        the live rock
Worship the dark bowels
        of the cold caves
Worship the high places
        steep as climbing
Worship the deeps
    the steeps

                    the steps
                         the scars
     Worship the grey rock
                    the granite rock
     the deep fissures
          in the cleft rock
     the rooks' nests
          in the cliff face
     the fossils forged
          in the chill air
     Worship the lofty dizziness
        where man rocks
     lullabied against the wind-swept broken boughs
        dangling perpendicular against
          the falling screes
     inconsequential in the chill air
        like uprooted trees

I lived in deepest Somerset for many years, spent countless hours in Cheddar Gorge, climbing its rocks and crags from the outside, plumbing the depths of its caves where the viscera is filled with stalactites that are the eighth wonder of the world. The scale of Nature cannot be reduced to language, any more than can its emotional impact. Many times I went to Cheddar with my camera, thinking a photograph might capture what words could not. But the camera fails too. Cheddar is not the Grand Canyon, nor Timna, nor the Yarlung Zangbo of China, nor the Kali Gandaki of Tibet, nor the Cotahuasi of Peru, nor the Copper Canyon of Mexico, but if you cannot get to any of these, go to Cheddar. If the universe has a pulse, this is one of the places where you can hear it beating.

Homage To William Shakespeare

The wisest fool in Christendom was old
and tired of such hypocrisy, the lies
that drove poor Timon out into the cold,
that led Macbeth his own life to despise.
No more the shadows of the candle's flame,
the fawning children and the relative
obscurity, just thirty-seven plays
and sonnets to a form superlative,
plus handbills from all his old productions,
tributes sent from Marston, Lyle and Jonson,
that battered box of grease-paints (slightly damp)
inherited by will of William Kemp.
Yet all of these no joy to him could bring –
not least the commendation from the King.

Such were the reliques of a life now used,
a mind which out of chaos order weaved,
a heart whole dedicated to the Muse
(the fame he had aspired to, and achieved).
There, on the desk before him, his life's work,
the last botched masterpiece, the folio
and quarto manuscripts (dead letterwork!
wisdom from the mouth of some Malvolio!).
All of this fugue and toil, this lucid heart,
this slow progress of thought and soul and Art,
this scorn, this vision that dissolved in rain,
this scroll on which he'd proudly scratched his name.
This to a man's whole Life and Will attested –
yet did not even know that he existed.

"Early Poems, "Japanese Poems", "Hebrew Poems" – how dull and unpoetical the titles of my earliest collections! Informative perhaps, but surely a work of poetry should be poetic everywhere, in every way it can. "Khaki On Both Sides" was definitely an improvement; "Coins" at least contained a pun; "The Pulse" certainly beat with the right intention, but it was my 2003 collection, "The Strings On The Dome Of The Tortoise" that made the leap – a very slow leap, as is appropriate for tortoises. To what does it allude? To the manner of constructing a lute in the ancient world, when Homer and King David were entertaining kings and gods. The original was probably the Persian "rud", which became the Arabic "ud", but while later instruments were made of wood, the earliest were quite simply large tortoise-shells attached by strings to a pegboard. The other early instrument of accompaniment was the lyre, which was really a small harp. The Greeks called a poem set to music a "lyric" because it was accompanied by a lyre, exactly parallel to that modern Orpheus Bob Dylan with his guitar hammering out the chords of "Hollis Brown" or "The Man In The Long Black Coat".

Retort To Adorno, Berlin, 2002

The rivers are ice.
The earth marshals its frigid strength,
brown with over-cultivation.
From East to West and West to East
the streets unite in Christmas lights and tinsel.
Postcards of the city
show a Wall, a rifle-toting sentry, a field of mines,
but all of this is history.
The Reichstag, now refurbished, re-inhabited,
warms the seat of future European government.
The marching feet on Unter den Linden and Alexanderplatz
stamp only to shake off the snow.
The Neue Synagogue (new in 1866)
may now be just a sad museum,
but down the road the Judische Gymnasium is full,
the Holocaust Memorial a dream of Albert Speer,
and in the little theatre in the Hackesches-Hoef
Jews full of Hechsher-Hofen mispronounce the name
while a Swiss Jew from Narbonne who looks like Tevya
plays the accordion in kletzmer style
and sings a kleine liedele in Yiddish
for the assembled ranks of Judeophile non-Jews.
When the show is done I approach him at the bar in Hebrew,
thank him for the Warshawsky rendering of Oseh Shalom
and the several encores and the explanations of the songs.
We talk in shrugs, as Jews have always done,
an arm raised this way indicates the Brandenburg Tor,
a shoulder that way points out Hitler's Bunker
on the Friedrich Strasse, two hundred metres
from the monument to Checkpoint Charlie on Rozinthaler Street.
Two hundred metres from Oranienburg Strasse
where the death of Jewry was proclaimed
a generation and a half ago,
the Swiss Jew and the English Jew shake hands,
exchange addresses,
bid shalom,
concur in parting that it is we who won.

Theodor Adorno (1903-1969) was a German philosopher and social critic. In 1949 he pronounced the dictum that "to write poetry after Auschwitz is barbaric", which was really intended as a challenge to his fellow-Germans, posing the profound question of what German culture could mean, or be, after the Holocaust. He later revised the dictum, stating that "perennial suffering has as much right to expression as a tortured man has to scream". He died too young to be familiar with the work of Max Sebald, and was probably unaware of the work of Heinrich Böll, but he was a close friend of Paul Celan; all three are writers who took up the Adorno challenge in their own ways, as did Günter Grass, who is acknowledged for doing so in a poem later in this collection. This "Retort To Adorno" is not a criticism, in the way the poems "Vergangenheitsbewältung" and "Der Gewöhnliche Deutsche" most definitely are; but for a Jew in Berlin, staring at the eagle still dominant above the Reichstag, and hearing the same old national anthem still playing, even though they no longer officially sing the words, it seemed the right title, and the right approach. The poem "Warsaw Pilgrimage" is really a continuation of this retort, if not actually of this poem. My story "Hunting Doughnuts In Berlin", in the collection "Travels In Familiar Lands", completes the trilogy.

9TH July 1995

I note that the first World Conference
of people in contact with Extra-Terrestrials
has been convened in Costa Rica

First, may I raise objection to my personal exclusion
I have tried repeatedly to talk to extra-terrestrial beings
and do not see why I should be disbarred
simply on the grounds that I have failed
where you claim to have succeeded

In my absence may I nonetheless request
that those of you who are in touch with ETs
pass on the following vital piece of information

that we are very keen to make friends with them
but only if they accept democracy
the absolute sanctity of Christian marriage
American goods guns films and pop music
a total ban on abortion and gay marriage
join the fight against pollution
allow us to mine their oil and other minerals
and boycott the State of Israel

Please can you also make it clear
to avoid any embarrassing misunderstanding
of these complex scientific and philosophical determiners
that we on earth are an intelligent life-form
which is not by any means the same thing
as an intelligent species

Is poetic chronology different from any other? I ask only because, as the reader may have noticed, this poem is dated 1995, where the previous was dated 2002. The answer has nothing to do with the logic of either time or poetry, but simply with the logic of book-publishing: I wanted to begin the collection with the Adorno poem, in order to set a tone for the volume. But it raises an interesting question about the ways in which we read poetry in and out of context. The intrinsic meaning of a poem is unchanged by that context, but our extrinsic understanding of it may very well be.

Poem That Could
For Example
Be Entitled
"Last Thoughts On
Monica Lewinsky"

The real point about his constant infidelities
is that he may have been unfaithful often
even very often
and even with an infinitude of women

But the one to whom he was unfaithful
was always and uniquely the same one
the same one all his life
from virginity to impotence the same one

And that
it must be said
is itself a kind of faithfulness

Passover, London, April 2003

Visiting my parents is an experience of death,
of many deaths in truth,
but least of all the future deaths,
the orphan deaths,
the would he want me to say Kaddish deaths,
the still-looked-good at ninety-two my grandmother deaths.

My father likes to dramatise his theoretic suicides
and give the reasons why he never would,
arguing treasons but not admitting cowardices,
while his own deaths gather round him like lost relatives:
his broken arm, missed opportunities, books read
in the days when he still read books,
a case of Barrett's oesophagus,
all the things he might have done,
or should have known but didn't know
(my lousy education or my sister doing drugs).
Death by nostalgia and regrets
and deafness.

Between the chopped liver and the boiled knaidloch,
my mother issues orders,
battalions of waitresses and cleaning ladies,
butlers, chauffeurs, removal men, wine tasters,
whole squadrons of flower arrangers, repairmen,
buffs to boss and underlings to hire and fire,
each the recipients of her constantly changing orders,
and each of them, all hundred of them,
incorporated in my father
or my sister if she's visiting to share the toil.
What dies is the disorder in the world,
reduced to ironed smoothness in a cupboard,
rearranged a hundred times and never ever right.

Death surrounds them in a hundred other forms:
the gerontospice they inhabit,
luxury 3-bedroom en-suite wards
for the privately self-financing.
Lawns die of over-manicuring and keep-off signs.

Flowers die of being looked at with a hunter's eye,
potential trophies for a cut-glass vase.
Paths die, aerated too often by golf-shoe spikes.
Religion dies of neglect.
Families die of suffocation.
Ambition and aspiration die of retirement.
There is nothing left alive – not even love,
dead from the neck upwards
as far as humanity is concerned,
from the heart inwards
by this stage of longevity;
and as to the desiccated organs –
these too are buried now
alongside nostalgia and regret.

Visiting my parents is an experience of death
in one very particular particular,
the solemn ritual moment in which
my father leads me to the cupboard,
leads me to the ceremony of the cupboard,
as though he were the Rabbi
and I the Bar Mitzvah boy.
This is where everything you need to know
is written down, he tells me,
pointing with his silver finger at the parchment.
Names of solicitors and accountants – long dead.
Numbers of bank accounts – already liquidated.
Copies of redundant wills.

You'll live another twenty years I promise him.
I hope not comes back the inexorable reply.
And from the kitchen a grand-daughter's voice
upbraiding grandma:
It's dark and gloomy as a coffin grandma,
meaning her own new flat in fact,
but in the circumstances every metaphor
risks adding certainty to certainty,
and in this life – my father's favourite platitude –
there is but one uncertainty
and that is when the inevitable will happen.

A Flower For STC

In my dreams at night
I travel immense distances -
further than Edom
farther than the Land of Nod -
and when I awaken in the morning
I am tired and dusty
my eyes are tired and dusty
and saliva from a spent shema
upon my lips

Bites from tropical mosquitoes
fester on my arms and legs
a scab from some dull scimitar
draws moons across my wrists
my legs are bent from walking
I - my heart - my soul
all bent from walking
and splinters from the wood
I have to drag

Where now - now that I am
where you sent me?
Where - now I am departed?
Where - now I have arrived?
Where now and then
where now?

In my dreams at night
I travel immense distances -
farther than yesterday
further than the world to come.
Today I came back with
a map of Heaven
out-of-date since the restoration
and the Rose of Paracelsus
faded past its best

Morality Test

You see a man drowning,
    in a storm, in a stream, in a flood.

Water terrifies you.

You are late.

You can see blood.

Do you dive in,
    risk your own death to save his?

Do you call for help,
    inviting others to be heroes?

Do you walk on by,
    unnoticing,
    knowing he would do the same for you?

And is your answer different,
    because he is Black,
    or Gay,
    or Jew?

STC, to save you the trouble of looking it up, was Samuel Taylor Coleridge, who wrote, imagining himself as Paracelsus, "If a man could pass through Paradise in a dream, and have a flower presented to him as a pledge that his soul had really been there, and if he found that flower in his hand when he awake — Aye! and what then?"

Ecce Homo

I am Christ, watching, listening.
Not *the* Christ,
but Christ by a follower of Dieric Bouts -
Flemish school, born 1415, Haarlem;
"Christ Crowned With Thorns" the eponym -
crucified, or painted, circa 1475,
the last regenerative act of both our lives.
Christ in a red smock
with shouldered ringlets for payot;
a noble Christ
unvanquished by death,
neck tendons taut as nails,
the pose heroic without hubris -
Christ as I would wish to be depicted
except for the crown of thorns,
composed, it seems, of coral,
or some stale marzipan purchased in the Arab souk
behind the Via Dolorosa,
green as moss upon a static stone;
and all these tears,
crystallised, caramelised, an excess of tears,
tears designed to rise to pathos
but falling - as tears should - to bathos,
pouring from the stigmata of over-bloodshot eyes.
The other Christ -
a Della Francesca by the languid look of him,
all alabaster arms and skin like frankincense -
the Christ on the far wall,
(my altar ego, if you'll forgive the pun),
some Tuscan fresco disimmured,
some Italianate triptych in the taste of Monte Cassino;
he does not watch the world, as I do,
he looks away -
histir panav, the Rabbis call it,
turning His countenance aside and letting evil enter -
two blind eyes like Pontius Pilate's,
two tearlessly white eye-sockets
turned inwards on his self-absorption,
a God of insipid Love,

self-love,
a God more focused on his inner pain
than on the boredom of eternity
or the careworn need for solace of humanity.
Not me.
I am all face.
Two open eyes, staring at you, judging.
Countenance turned to shine on you,
to be, and bear, your burden.
Watching. Listening.

*

The tears though are not mine - I never cried -
but each artist has the right
to paint his personal Crucifixion.
The tears are for you, my modern worshippers.
How shall I address you?
In the modern style, in slogans, soundbites?

You, the canons of commercialism
(or do I mean the clerics? the communicants?),
pacing in reverential silence
the wood-floored cloisters of this Courtauld Gallery
(it was never like this in the Temple -
all blood and bartering,
all stench of zealotry and incense;
but usury is still usury;
I still dream of driving the merchants from the marketplace).
You, the mendicants of materialism,
the bored, the pseud, the popish, the pontificating,
the bedesmen and the iconolaters,
(the death of God is a death in language too,
words genizahed like the Word itself).

You, the awe-struck and the fascinated,
the pious and the pompous -
all Mankind eventually walks before me.
You who have come here for a space of silence in the city,
for a stamp in the passport
of your journey towards adulthood,
to venerate Madonna for her line and form,

125

the angels for their chiaroscuro,
the saints for their grisaille,
the benefactors for the sheer scale of their benefactions,
the messianic Cortauld for his model of munificence...
You came to pass judgments, didn't you?
Well I, Christ, I too came to judge.
Along with forgiveness and the shouldering of sin,
this is my designated role,
this eaves-dropping on your secret conversations,
this being an icon on your wall,
this watching as a mirror watches,
this reflecting you back upon yourselves,
this making my judgements upon your judgements,
I, the helmsman of your inner voyage,
witness,
scapegoat,
paradigm of paradise,
Ecce Homo.

                           *

Eternity in this underworld yields to deep thinking
(forgive these digressions;
I so rarely get the chance to speak
and one thought feeds another
as my teacher Rabbi Gamliel once said).

I am struck (for example)
that a gallery hosts paintings without contexts,
so a picture becomes a sculpture,
an object frozen in time and space,
integral only to itself,
shorn of its narrative and its relationships,
displaced,
reduced - yes, I'm sure I do mean that - to eternity.
Gone the votive candles, the ringing angelus,
the susurrations from confession booths,
the ambient Gregorian, the pacing priests,
the hammering of nails into the master masonry
as builders pave the spiral path to God
(O but I love these puns - reliques,
in the style of midrash, of my Rabbinic training;

though you no doubt would call them Joyceian).
We who anyway were just
the mediaeval Piagetian paraphernalia of prayer
(that's the sort of language game I mean;
Kohelet and King David would have been applauding;
the Word, they would have said,
is still alive, original, incarnate),
the atmosphere-engendering wall-hangings,
the aides to spiritual intensity
and the adornments of some Lady Chapel,
we are all that now remains,
hung in the wrong Temple,
icons to the wrong divinities,
prayers unpronounceable,
mere Art.
Gone the flesh - we are the bones.
Gone the edifice - we are the ruins.
Gone the intent - we are the intensities.
In place of God - Man.
And which side of that equation will you place me on?
Aye, there's the rub!

*

I am less racked by nails here
than ever I was on Calvary.
One stabbed through my back, like Judas,
and then the rope he also used to hang himself;
but here I hang much longer
than those three short hours of eternity.
Here I hang all day and every day
(except, of course, Bank Holidays and Christmas -
a charming irony),
tormented Jesus, scourged and speared,
though perhaps the torment you are witnessing
is less my torment
than the epiphany of the artist's torment
in the making of me
(I mean, of course, the earthly artist,
not the divine creator)...
I wonder if those modern picklers in vinegar,
those dadaists of the formaldehyde cow,

also took their cue from Roman sponges?
Nor is this quite the underworld I had expected,
though it is subterranean enough,
gloomy as a Yom Kippur yeshiva.
It lives, of necessity, in limited daylight,
in shadows cast by chandeliers,
a deliberate absence of illumination.
(Here is a most Scholastic paradox:
too much light would harm the surfaces;
too much light also reveals too much interior).
The walls are deadened by paint and fingerprints
(the paint the same green as my thorns),
by the conflicting echoes of adjacent paintings
(I must say I find it rather disconcerting
to be surrounded by so many and such nude Madonnas),
and little white plaques
(mine no doubt reads IMRI)
like labels on a jar of Scopus olives
(thirty shekels pitted, more with stones).
This is no longer living Art
(though the Psalmist would adore my echo-lines,
my use of the parenthesis as counterpoint).
This is a shop of shadows,
a sarcophagus entombed in a museum
(the Italian who said that
looked a lot like Cerberus himself).
This is history
become theme-park.
And though I long to have the rock rolled back,
to make hejira from this whiteless sepulchre,
the truth is
that you cannot steal my body from this tomb
because the eye of God protects it on closed circuits,
the arms of God contain it
in a grip invisible that screams at any touch,
(I have often wondered
how far history would have been affected
had Joseph of Arimathea
taken these same precautions at his tomb);
why, even my eternal corpus
is kept at mummy temperature by humidifiers,
though doubts have been expressed by certain Thomases

over the radioactive damage of electric light.
But I am safe here,
enwombed and entombed,
no longer living Art nor living God,
no longer myth nor legend;
but an item in a catalogue,
a world-wide web-site,
the apotheosis
now
of the profit
not the Prophet.
I can't say it's the worst fate
that ever befell Man or God.

                    *

In the upstairs rooms -
Lely, Sassoferrato, Rubens, Brueghel -
religion is replaced by human vanity,
which is to say veneration for the Creator
by the cult of the created,
art purloined into the service of self-aggrandisement,
the great (and especially the smaller would-be great),
the good (and generally the genuinely not-that-good),
crying like tormented Jesuses:
"O me! O look at me!"
from a gilt frame twice life-sized.
Marvellous paintings - but at what price?
"I am Lorenzo Lotto by your leave..."
(you would need to win the lotto to acquire him!);
but in truth he is a gloomy, melancholy man,
not unlike my master Hillel
or that glum, dejecting John the Baptist,
all charcoal and ashes,
Jeremiac black on a black background -
and note the humanising skull
in the bottom left-hand corner,
hinting at Calvary-Golgotha, the Hill of Skulls,
but failing, in ebony and ravens,
even to tilt a nod at Resurrection.
Or take the works of Thomas Gainsborough
on the floor below the room of the Impressionists

(I have no gripe about Impressionism -
all that light, that life-enhancing, Mediterranean light),
but Gainsborough,
a synonym for Mammon if there ever was one,
alabaster plagiarised no doubt from the Della Francesca,
all those porcine porcelain faces,
all that Hanoverian photographic art
informed by the slow aperture and fast shutter techniques
of Anthony Van Dyck.
Idolatry! Graven images! Treyf!
Blessed are the vain and wealthy
for they shall be transmuted into icons,
hung up for the edification of the servile classes,
masters and mistresses resplendent on the wall,
the lower castes cap-doffing in the gallery...
What is extraordinary is only that the Gainsboroughs
are not portrayed in red smocks,
with shouldered ringlets,
their fingers counting rosaries,
and crucifixes on their nail-taut tendons.

*

Five o'clock approaches,
time to shut up this shop of shadows.
Today, alone, I have watched four thousand of you,
hajis circling round and round the black-stone walls
of this false Temple filled with diptychs, triptychs,
altar-pieces, icons, frescos,
with plaster imitations of erstwhile marbles,
and for some reason ivories and faiences from Limoges
(the sacred art of Europe, 1300-1500,
so it says upon the door);
I have watched you, listened to you,
I, "Christ Crowned With Thorns",
and you, uncertain how to celebrate this shrine of God-in-Art
and I confess
(I never did to Caiaphas, but will to you)
I am as much bewildered as amused.
Why are you worshipping me here,
you who never visit me at home,
you who never bend the knee,

you who never sing the litany or liturgy?
Why - what form of indulgence are you seeking?
You who study the semiotics of the labels
in order to glean the semiotics of the paintings,
reading the easier of what you think
are two parts of the same work,
learning a name, a date, a brief interpretation,
believing, with most perfect faith,
that now you understand,
that now you can speak with confidence
at dinner with the intellectuals,
that now you have achieved
a kind of symbiosis with the divine.
And what if I were to tell you
(I always was a rebel, a discomforter)
that my label is all wrong,
that I am neither IMRI
nor "Christ by a follower of Dieric Bouts",
but Bouts himself, that follower of Van der Weyden,
that I am not 1475 but actually 1463,
that I am only a cartoon for the Resurrection
hung - yes, hung - in the Munich Pinakothek?
Would all that data cause transfiguration
in your lack of understanding of me?
You who would take home the memory
of this rare occasion of intensity,
a photograph,
a thread from my cloak or shroud,
a postcard,
a relic,
a souvenir.
You who speak of the great value of these paintings,
and mean capital,
not culture.
You who read the donors' plaques
as iconistically as you read the labels on the paintings.
You who are enamoured by the names of names
(but not the Name),
and do not understand philanthropy,
like Art,
is best left egoless?
Why, why are you here?

How Logic Can Defeat The Barbarians

Ultimately the barbarians cannot achieve their goal
because we the intellectuals
can defeat them every time in matters of perception.
When they burn our books
we will know that they have made us
carbon copies

Love, Or Art

Love or Art:
an empty space in head or heart;
the eye, the hand, the soul, the mind,
first yearn, then fill the space, to find
the emptiness no longer waste,
and need, and yearning, both displaced.

Ode On Suffering

While I was screaming in agony
you were watching the television
and not the news bulletin in which they mentioned me
but the soap opera on the other channel

While I was lying in a pool of my own blood
you were salting the breast of a spring chicken
cleaning out its guts and gizzard
chopping garlic for the gravy

While my bones were being broken
you stubbed your little toe on the foot of the bed
and from the fuss you made
it could have been the end of the entire universe

While I was burning to death
you were rewiring a lampshade

While I was dripping mucus from my mouth and nose
you were shopping for cosmetics

While I was coughing flakes of tissue from my lungs
you were lying in the bath relaxing

While I was being murdered
you were getting over a squabble with the neighbours
or writing
or reading
this poem

Forget Job and the wager made by God and Satan
Forget all the rhetoric and polemic and theological explication
This, this is the true nature of human suffering

An ephemeron
An incidence of bathos and banality

For Philip Larkin

The graffiti on the library wall in Hull said simply:
"Pornography is not sex - but hatred"
which left me wondering what the librarian himself would say
given his personal propensities

That desire (perhaps) is kindled by sunsets, art and landscapes
in exactly the same manner
in exactly the same measure
as that aesthetic phenomenon called Woman

That watching humans copulate
is neither more nor less erotic
neither more nor less unnatural
than watching gibbons at the zoo.

That anyway desire is not for sex itself
but symbiosis
an epiphany of the human soul
the word made flesh
a return to some original
primordial
hermaphroditic status
the pursuit of androgyny
through the other

                    *

Larkin is presumably a variant of Larrikin
Australian for the sort of rowdy hooligan
who scrawls graffiti on a library wall
whether in vulgar words or accurate anatomies
a veritable Whitsun wedding of the sacred and profane

Also, more obliquely,
but in the style of the librarian,
a derivative of laverock,
itself a variant of loverock,
from the olde aenglish laferce and the middle dutch lewerike,
a sandy-brown feathered horny skylark with long hind-claws

and its own propensity for daubing on a library wall

What would the loverock say of this?
That the artist paints it
that the poet turns it into ode
that the lover makes love to it
but that the enigma remains enigma
and possession of "the thing itself" utterly elusive
whether in word or photograph or flesh

That where one cannot possess beauty
there grows up envy
That where one cannot dispel envy
there grows up hatred
That where one cannot subdue hatred...

                    *

No, the moral graffitist was correct
Pornography is not about sex
not even about watching men have sex with women
not even about watching women have sex with women
nor any other combination permutation

It is about the abuse of beauty
by the dispossessed
not hatred necessarily
but a turning of sex into ugliness
by the ugliness of the pornographer
a spoiling of the Whitsun wedding

It is the self-same process
in fact
as he who cannot really read or write
daubing graffiti on a library wall

Besides being one of Britain's most respected poets, Philip Larkin
was, for many years, the librarian at Hull University; he also
became, posthumously — not so much famous as an object of
prurience, when his interest in pornography was discovered.

Silence

Silent, silent, little poet
Do not speak it though you know it
Do not whisper, do not roar
What the world will just ignore

Do not sing it, do not show it
Do not plant it, do not grow it
Do not sculpt, no, do not draw
What the world has no use for

In the eaves beneath the roof
Hide the evidence of Truth
In the finitude of skies
In the sanctuary of Lies

Silent, silent, little poet
In the darkness safely stow it
In the quiet of the hold
Where the word cannot be told

The scansion of this poem unconsciously reflects both Blake's "Tiger, Tiger" and Jane Taylor's plagiarism of the French "Ah! vous dirai-je maman", which she called "Twinkle Twinkle Little Star", and which Mozart published as his "Twelve Variations" (K265/300e); both J.C.F. Bach and Joseph Haydn had already used the melody, as would Camille Saint-Saens later in the 12th movement of the "Carnival of the Animals". The version by Franz Liszt (S.163b) is probably the closest of all these to the scansion of my poem, though this, as I say, is entirely fortuitous and coincidental.

Beauty

She came from nowhere
  had nothing
no pedigree no class no status,
no education money family contacts
but she was
  o most exquisitely
        a beauty

Gradually, inevitably
the privileges of beauty flowered in her

a husband with aristocratic cousins
the status of a diplomat's wife
  in the highest echelons of government
access to books teachers
wise men sophisticated friends
money
  and still more money
the confidence of presidents artists intellectuals

Then she reached sixty
  the age when beauty fades
and she knew
  what no one else knew
that she who now had everything
  once more also had nothing

A Poem For The Equidies

I have found, in an encyclopaedia
of some considerable obscurity
the sort of thing I never learned
in school in normal classes

Apparently in China
in 1200 CE
some shaman when his eyes got burned
invented the sunglasses

Two Become One

Two lovers sit together in a room,
on a bed where they have inhabited
the intimacy of each other's body.

They read their own copy of the same book,
the same page of the same chapter,
each absorbed in the same plot,
each hearing the same music
on the radio in the background

each occupying an entirely separate universe.

The View From Hispaniola

From the distance we could see the boats,
so much like our boats but with mis-shapen sails,
the Spanish flag waving from the crow's nest,
the long black cannons and the thirsty sailors,
the soldiers emerging from the bowels to come ashore,
the planting of the flag, first, then the Cross,
the kissing of the sandy soil,
the cheering of their chief as he addressed them,
the unloading of food,
the starting to build shelters.

At last, after all these centuries,
our messages must have gotten through,
our invitation to the unknown white men
to come and share our paradise.

At last they can be silenced,
all those who doubted
there was human life beyond these shores.

At last, at last,
we have discovered Europe.

Lines Of Latitude

Where I grew up we lived like AmerIndians
at the point where two roads forked
two quiet roads loved without reservation
revered since pre-Columban times
milestones for Dick and Cat
traced all the way from Gloucestershire to Dover -
until the cowboys came and built a flyover

First they drove a dual carriageway
along our narrow lane
two perfect parallel lines
like the tram-lines of a suburban lawn
manicured couplets of suburban poetry
mowed by Sir John Bitumen in careful rows
like Surrey stockbrokers on a golfless Sunday morning

Then they ploughed a metal furrow down the middle -
a scale model in blue steel of the Berlin Wall
only far more dangerous to try to cross it -
designed to stop us getting to the freedom of the park
now marked out for development

So Brook Lane gave way to Nelson Mandela Avenue -
the mis-spelled Brooke remembered less as a Great War poet
than as a sewage problem -
and thence to Oak Tree Drive
the ancient oak emblazoned
as the logo of a rather tacky pub
done out in panels of reconstituted sawdust
from what may very well have once been oak
and a green baize on its pool table
putting green as opposed to jade or emerald
as smooth as astro-turf

Yokels are now called locals
the park remains a park
but now for cars

*

All that was thirty years ago
before the still point of the turning world
was redefined
as a seven mile traffic jam along the Watford Way
before the interminable necropolis stretched
so far beyond the doors of our new-made suburbia
that we were now labelled "inner city"
by the posses riding bareback on the flyover

Interminable necropolis
crossed by a bridge too near
forty miles east to west
thirty miles north to south
though you cannot reduce to mere arithmetic
to grid references
what are the deeper lines of human longitude

Longitude - not latitude
Cities on the scale of London
afford the human soul no latitude

On Poems And Poetry

With some modern poetry
one never really knows
if what one is reading
is not really prose

Now all men can write poems
or doggerel or verse
though most men do it badly
while others do it worse

For a poem's just a thing of words
and images and lines
and sometimes it has rhymes as well
but other times it doesn't.

The Japanese counted the syllables
The Romans built on trochees and dactyls
Shakespeare used iambic pentameters
Byron was born in 1788
Wilfred Owen positively explodes
 with alliterative onomatopoeia -
so much for the schoolmasterly approach

Any real poet will tell you
there is no such thing as
blank verse

                    *

Now sometimes a poem
        isn't a poem at all
                but a piece of word art
        sculpted on a page

Formless
        structureless
                    one line
ending
through some arbitrary preference

when one word sooner
    or later
  would not have made much
  difference
(and it was really intended to be prose, only the line
didn't quite reach the end of the page)

Or a poem can be a thing of streaming consciousness
  similes as if pouring out of the human brain
   (the likeable and dislikeable human brain)
     soft as rancid butter
       sweet as lemon juice
the Muse-of-Shakespeare stimulated
 tedious drone of metaphors
   profound as any wadi

                    *

So much for poems
But poetry
poetry is a living thing
that winces if you press too hard
and shivers in the cold of anger
and feels and makes you feel
and loves because it knows love
because it has touched the heart of hatred
and come through it
a thing that grows
and grows
and goes on growing
even after the poet has ceased growing
a thing that never turns to stone
not even in the dull mind
not even in the unbeating heart
not even in the soul of stone
a thing that knows nothing
of mortality or immortality
but if you prick it
it bleeds

The Soul Loves To Swim
(for PW)

He drove his cart between the two big stringybarks
and stopped
became the dominant tree in that part of the bush
rose above the involved scrub
with the simplicity of true grandeur
put down roots

He had long ago abandoned all the trivia
all those tepid pursuits of the tame shore-huggers
fringed with leaves
those timid Australians of the soul
for whom there are just two worlds
a pair of shoes with leather soles
and leather inners
worn the right foot hugging the white coast
unworn the left foot pointed to
but only pointed to
the aboriginal heart and hinterland
and fools like Leichardt-Voss
fording the safe umbilicus between

He had, I say, abandoned all the trivia
the clear rock-pool
the picnic-hampered beaches
the paddle-boats
the ankle-dippers
women covered up or barely topless
red-skin men with handkerchiefs for feathers
the neat bourgeois mahogany monotony
the wife and one point nine-to-five-thirty children
the trimmed privet private keep out hedge -
had made a tent of sky upon the sand
and mortgaged it to hazard

and now
if only for tonight
if only transient ephemeral
behold the gorgeous coral reef

the black and naughty spikes of sea-urchins
the luminescent jelly-fish
unkosher prawns

lying on the beach
reading of all unlikely things
a book of my own poems
strange vanity
unaware of who it is that passes by
and caring less
for authors are another aspect
of the very trivialities he has abandoned
authors are men who scribble books and poems
whereas this is poetry

So he reads
"sea anemones
fractions of light broken on the sea's mirror"
and
"ladders of sea-weed"
and
"the sun's white candle"

The soul loves to swim -
or float
which is another form of balance -
whether between the stringybarks
or on the sea-shell floor
though at his age and stage of health
floating belly-up would be the easiest

but belly-down it is
eyes wide open on the marvellous
marvellous secrets of this underwater world
while them on the hotel patios and promenades
them sipping coke or crunching candy-floss
them safe for beaching on dry land
them safer still for holiday insurance schemes
and paying on the VISA

and him out there
a dead body apparently

plathicarus primordiensis
"washed up astounded on the white white beach"
belly and face buried in the water
hair of sea-sponge
flesh of sea-horse
nothing trivial here
a tree of man
a corpse
a genesis

For Theodor Herzl, May 2001

By the stream of Ban-ar-Well
I sit and weep for what has happened to Jerusalem
How men are hung like harps upon its willows
Men singing the songs of captives in a strange land
Men with too much cunning in their right hands
Men who speak through tongue-cleaved palates
Men who are only really happy
dashing the little ones upon the rocks

Rase it, rase it, to the very foundations
Reward the man who sets fire to the veil

Then build a new city
Not with walls and visions
But with living souls

Relativity

Travelling against the time-clock
travel itself steals time
five full hours on this occasion
ten a.m. at take-off
two p.m. when the sun begins to set
as though the plane's acceleration
hastened time's passing
each minute five minutes
and the sun retreating westwards

Toronto was tiny from the air
like all cities
but not London
usually seen at blinking-pace
between low cloud and the runway

Today in cloudless skies
and circling to await a landing call
its very immensity was startling
from Windsor Toy Castle
to the scale model of London Bridge

Even without the excuse of jet-lag
I doubt Wordsworth could have made
a better poem than the place itself
nor Einstein demonstrated the matter better

The Sketch

All my life I have wanted to draw
to make perfect images and likenesses
the way the God of Creation did

But what I make are marks
infantile marks
the blemishes of a wobbly hand
smearing its uncertainties

Gradually one learns
that shading is more precise than lines

Gradually one learns
not to draw eyes, nose, mouth
but the darkness underneath the lip
the hollows cavitied by light
the depths of orifices
the parts that make two dimensions
three dimensional

Yet the hand goes on wobbling
Lines on the inner eye miss their target
End products are images but never likenesses
still human beings
        but expressed as inexactitudes

Warsaw Pilgrimage

Like a tourist in Jerusalem
who goes straight to the Western Wall,
my starting-point the Nozykow Synagogue on Twarda Street,
the south-easternmost corner of the ghetto sixty years ago
and now, again, in use, if only half-restored,
the heating off in minus eight degrees
to meet the deadline of a grant.

Shabbat is in a half an hour already
before we have a minyan,
the Rabbi in New York for a conference,
his deputy in the maternity ward
where his wife, mazal tov,
is producing a shobbas baby.

The local yeshiva boy who leads the prayers
is a cousin of that pianist Szpilman
in Roman Polanski's movie;
he has to compete with Moshe the Dwarf,
a brash Israeli who prefers his own nusach,
but we get through Yedid Nephesh
and Lecha Dodi without a fight,
and anyway, we in the pews agree to disagree,
Judaism always was a dialectic of agreements
and disagreements.

Afterwards the twenty-five of us who prayed
are doubled by the twenty-five who didn't
for a community meal as the guests of Estée Lauder.
Members of the Foundation
sit opposite members of the Joint
and argue, but harmoniously,
about why there is no one there from ORT.
Noise, disagreement,
melodies in counterpoint but everybody singing.
This, this is how a Jewish community is grown.

*

My Warsaw streetfinder points out roads and alleys
missing from my Warsaw Ghetto plan
and vice versa.
The shul was on the Twarda, then as now,
but the school next-door, the Lauder-Joint,
was then the ORT school, square and courtyarded,
where all that's left today is flat and destitute.

Flats and destitution make up all the ghetto,
where it is not entirely open space and trees,
the Muranow by name, sliced through the middle
by al Solidarnosci,
tribute to several liberations further on than ours.
At the junction of Anielewicza and the Zamenhofa
stands the monument of the ghetto fighters,
a fraction of the scale of that other monument
to that other uprising,
the one in which the blade-sharpeners
rose up against the butchers
hoping to free the city before the arrival of those
who would exchange the butchers' knives for scimitars.
All we have is a metal board
lost amid the snow, the space, the trees,
announcing plans to one day build a monument,
a museum to the Polish Jews;
after which, presumably, they will feel free
to reckon the real-estate value of the urban park
and put up still more high-rises.

On Lewartowskiego, just beyond the ghetto shrine,
Willy Brandt the German Chancellor kneels in penance,
an absurd shrine to a most absurd apology,
and more absurd still the eighteen ancient stele,
carved in Hebrew hieroglyphs,
a Path of Remembrance that leads
beyond the ghetto gates to the Umschlagplatz,
whence 350,000 Jews were taken to that place
from which no apologies can ever come.

Pawla, Dzielna, Nowolipki, Zamenhofa, Ogrodowa.
The people have gone, their homes, their yellow stars,

the hatred that was felt for them, their hunger, squalor,
their humiliation – all of this is gone now sixty years.
But street-names where this happened have endured
and in that extraordinary fake the "Old Town",
rebuilt correct in every detail by the Soviets,
you can still purchase wooden carvings
of those vanished Jews,
dangling peyos, black gabardine, rabbinic fiddlers,
Polish Shylocks condemned by German Portias,
barterable down to sixty zlotys each –
the price of decent soap.
I bought an entire family –
mother, father, daughter, son –
and brought them home like kindertransport
the way Lourdes pilgrims
take home plastic holy-water bottles
in the image and the shape of Sister Bernadotte.

*

Snow freezes in the soul as well as in the veins.
By the third day of my visit I am sick of all this death,
have risen early to visit the new Jewish school,
to meet the leaders of the new Jewish youth club,
to see my former students who now live and work here,
one in Warsaw, two in Wroclaw, teaching Hebrew.
We take breakfast, strictly kosher,
in a coffee bar on Jerozolimskie (where else?)
and talk about their future.
They ask me, why have I never visited before,
and I try to tell them
they are the reason why I have never visited before
because they were not yet here, but only
the empty spaces in the Murowa, but only
the replica town and the wooden carvings, but only
the politically inspired apologies
and the grandiose monuments.
For forty years I did not visit
because one cannot justify a pilgrimage
into the past,
but only into the future.

After "The Strings On The Dome Of The Tortoise", the quest for titles for future volumes became self-competitive. I couldn't possibly revert to the banalities of the earlier collections; but where to find something worthy? "Strings" described the instrument of accompaniment, but what of the process of writing. I looked up the word "Muse" in the dictionary, and was surprised at myself for never having registered before, the connection between "Muse" and "Museum" – a museum in Greek means "a shrine to the Muses". But something about this also bothered me. In our world, a museum is a theme-park of history, a place where dead things are preserved. Though they may inspire the looker to create, their purpose is not creation, not even education, but simply storage. The intention may be a shrine, but at some level the outcome is a prison. A book of poems is precisely the same, a place where previous work can be gathered and displayed: a museum in miniature. And the poet, as well as the Muse, caged within. So the book became "The Caged Song-Bird Of The Muses".

For your information, there were Nine Muses in the ancient world: Calliope, goddess of epic poetry; Clio, goddess of history; Erato, goddess of lyric poetry; Euterpe, goddess of music; Melpomene, goddess of tragedy; Polyhymnia, goddess of choral poetry; Terpsichore, goddess of dance; Thalia, goddess of comedy; Urania, goddess of astrology. Interesting that there was no Muse of sculpture or fine art, though drama is implied, because it was an essential element of tragedy.

A Note In The Diary Of God

In the year 1897
the year in which her mother died
Elisabeth Nietzsche returned home from Paraguay
where she had been working
with her husband Bernhard Förster
to establish an Aryan
anti-Semitic German colony
known as Nueva Germania

Just outside the town of Röcken bei Lützen
in that farming district southwest of Leipzig
where she and her brother had been born
Elisabeth rented a large house on a hill
known as the Villa Silberblick
and moved her brother
with his collected manuscripts
and his diagnosis of incurable dementia
to the residence

This became the new home
of the Nietzsche Archives
previously located
at the family home in Naumburg
and here Elisabeth received visitors
who wanted to gawk at
or pay homage to
the now-incapacitated philosopher

On August 25, 1900
shortly before his 56th birthday
Friedrich Nietzsche succumbed
to pneumonia apparently
in combination with a stroke
His body was transported to the family gravesite
directly beside the church in Röcken bei Lützen
where his mother and sister now also rest

A plaque on the grave
inscribed with his name and dates
makes unequivocally clear
for all the world to see and understand
that the philosopher Nietzsche
spokesperson for Zarathustra
is
dead

Themes recur, as do good ideas, because one never really feels one has articulated them fully, and hopefully this time the words will come out right. Sometimes they recur for an entirely different reason – the same reason that one plants out the same flower-pots with geranium every year, that one returns again and again to the same restaurant, the same holiday beach, the same golf course, the same lover: because one never really feels that one has exhausted them.

A Romantic Love Poem

There was once a romantic love poem
desp'rate to get itself writ
it searched the world o'er for a poet
whose heart with love's fire had been lit

It hunted and hunted and hunted
but damn it, it couldn't find one
not in the west and not in the east
nor under the moon nor the sun

there were plenty of third-rate song-writers
there were dozens of crooners as well
but of poets whose hearts were a-blazing
not one between heaven and hell

So how could it hope to get written
o how could it hope to get home
to the lady whose fate was receiving
this refugee homeless love pome

O pity the words that were waiting
to be turned into lyric or ode
O pity the images fading
like love on the thorns of the rose

O pity the verse unrecited
the metaphors dearly bought
the rhymes at times disunited
the similes like this one unwrought

O pity the lady who's waiting
to hear what her love has to bring
but his lips have been blunted to silence
cause he can't find the tune he would sing

O pity the lover who's yearning
to tell of his love in a song
and the romance is def'nitely burning
but the verses just come out all wrong

There was once a romantic love poem
desp'rate to get itself writ
and it tried and it tried but unless I'm belied
I'm pretty damned sure this ain't it

Ode To Immortality

I feel sorry for you
Ludwig van Beethoven
not for your deafness
which had no impact on your music-making
but for that immortality
which keeps your name alive beyond your death

I feel sorry for you
Ludwig van Beethoven
because that immortality
which keeps your name alive beyond your death
is still not sufficient immortality
to have experienced Mahler, Rachmaninoff or Sibelius

After Reading Stephen Crane

A foul stench stank up the street today
something from the sewers probably
but it rose to the high heavens;
a foul stench like something putrefying,
something mouldering and decomposing,
meat from some butcher's shambles
or the alley behind some Chinese restaurant.

And then I realised,
when God died his body must have rotted too
the meat gone high, the organs putrefied;
it too would have stunk from the high heavens
right down to the celestial sewers.

But God is ancient, very ancient,
and it would have taken...
easily a hundred years;
and high heaven is a long way distant...
easily a hundred years
for all that stench to reach us on low Earth.

So this is what it must have been
not unsold poultry or stale chow mein
but this, this was the cause of the terrible stink;
it was the dead body of God, putrefying,
and foolish me
thinking it was the stench of human history.

I wish I could remember what Stephen Crane I was reading that set me off to write this, but I honestly cannot. I have checked my diaries, but there is nothing but this poem. I have looked him up on-line, and much enjoyed discovering that his first book of poems, "The Black Riders", was dismissed by the New York Tribune as "so much trash", to which another commentator added the weight of his ego with "there is not a line of poetry from the opening to the closing page; poetic lunacy would be a better name for the book." This is precisely the sort of encouragement we poets hope for from the critics; sadly the names of the two critics, and the collections of their reviews, have not survived into posterity. Crane's poetry has, though we may well choose to regard it as not being "sustained like his prose", the mere "refuse of his prose, the sawdust of his first-rate work", as per Richard Zenith's introduction to Fernando Pessoa (see page 3). Crane's response was to thank the critics for the free publicity; myself I prefer to send a postcard I have made in their honour, a poem of sorts, but also a nice picture to hang on their walls; it really is this simple:

Here are the tools. See if you can do better.

Regards, Prashker

And speaking of anagrams, of there being just twenty-six letters available for us to permute, into words, phrases, paragraphs, volumes...

All Our Diaries

All our diaries record the same thoughts
All our poems sing the same songs
All our dreams climb the same ladder
All our ambitions break their ankles on the same log

And if there really is nothing new under the sun
How may I go further?
How can I climb higher?

To answer this I have written for myself a motto
a question that no writer should ever need to answer:

How dare you write a book
That didn't change my life?

Cordelia's Lament

Somewhat too late
I realised
that love is not restricted
that love is not dispersed in finite quantities
and runs out when you use it up

A man can love his God
with all his heart and soul and might
and still have love left over
for his fellow-man

So too can a young woman
yearning for a husband
still speak the something
that is more than nothing

Love and be silent
Love more richer than my tongue
Love according to my bond
and more
and less

Somewhat too late
I realised
that love is like a pool of water
out of which a soul may drink
knowing the pool will be refilled
each time it storms upon the heath

Der Gewöhnliche Deutsche[1]

All of us subscribed
to the casual reorganisation
of history
Why did nobody protest?
All of us watched them
drag away the Jews and Gypsies
All of us collaborated
with our words or our silence
with our acts or our passivity
with our flight or our remaining
with our good eye or the blind one
All of us lost family and friends
All of us witnessed the devastation of our homeland
All of us knew that we were implicated
All of us evaded feeling guilty
Why did nobody
for nearly sixty years already
ever find the courage
to invent this poem?

I could have set this in Rwanda, or Armenia, in Damascus, or the Central African Republic, in North Korea or the Soviet Union, in Mao's China or Amritsar…the list is longer than the space available to write it, and the point made, hopefully, without needing to. In January 2014 I saw the movie "12 Years A Slave"; not being a movie buff I had no idea who the director was, though I foolishly assumed he was the same Steve McQueen who had starred in those epic masterpieces "The Towering Inferno" and "The Magnificent Seven". Exiting, I was about to comment to my companion that at last here was an American movie worth making, a serious movie on a serious subject, rather than the usual round of shoot-bang-fire fantasy or suburban heartbreak; but someone else said, "Why does it take a Brit to make a movie like this? Why can't we make our own movies, about our own past, and start to deal with it?" Now I wanted to say *Vergangenheitsbewältung*, but the word is difficult and my memory poor. Apparently the woman was quoting the movie's producer Brad Pitt.

---

[1] The word means "usual", "customary" or "ordinary".

The Board Hand-Over To The Administration

I told them it was a historic day
that they should be proud of themselves
for having the courage and the boldness
to take such a decisive and important step
acknowledging the maturity of the institution
that no longer requires such tight command

I told them it was the beginning of a new age
and would have had them sing something appropriate
to celebrate the moment
Moses' Shira at the crossing of the Red Sea perhaps
or rehearse the Hallel Psalms that we were meant to sing
the following morning in rejoicing at Rosh Chodesh

Bye bye Bye-laws would have made a lovely pun
but puns were not the order of the day
Simply I made the speech that was expected
and sat back gloating in the pleasure
of witnessing that o so rare event:
the voluntary resignation of authority and power

There Are Three Ways To Bake A Potato

There are three ways to bake a potato
You can put it in the microwave
for four minutes
or you can put it in a normal oven
for an hour and a half
or you can put it in a slow oven
overnight or overday
You get a perfectly good potato
from any of these three
but people who serve on committees
are wedded to the slow approach
so if you are attending a meeting
to discuss the baking of a potato
it is advisable to microwave your dinner first

For K

When the world of women is divided
between those born to be made love to
and those to be fallen in love with
I choose the side of K
who crossed the ravine at Babi Yar with me
but said she would never let me kiss her
tongue to tongue
until the both of us relented

Ah yes, poetry as obscurity! This one so obscure, I have absolutely no recollection whatsoever who K was, when I met her (or imagined her), or what the connection with Babi Yar might have been. I have never been to Babi Yar, though I have written about it in a novel, "Going To The Wall". K was a character in Franz Kafka's novel "The Trial", but I am fairly sure that K was a male and I know I have never kissed Kafka, though I did once stare adoringly into a photograph of him, in a shop window, in what had once been his house, in Prague. So the poem must remain obscure – but rather neat, and great fun, for all that.

One Evening In A Sad Café Off Yonge Street

Whatever happened to the blonde woman
with the amazingly long legs
who asked me to improvise a poem for her
one evening in a sad café off Yonge Street
and I wrote this poem?

Did she understand this poem was not a poem at all
but simply the manifestation
of a yearning to make love to her?
Did she recognise the intent behind my tone of voice
the desire upon my lips and fingers?

Did she take my hand and walk me home?
Or did she suddenly recall a morning meeting
the need to bathe and have an early night?

And either way, did she regret
the taken
or the neglected opportunity?

Who knows? Maybe this was K.

I Run From Domesticity

I run from domesticity as from a man with a pistol
   as you would run from a rapist with a knife

I see the pistol everywhere
   even in my dreams at night
I see a figure brandishing the pistol
     to make me sew up the holes in my sweater
     to order me to bake a coffee cake
     to coerce me into cleaning the bath I failed to clean
     to strong-arm me into disinfecting the kitchen table
     to require me to put the garbage out
        and then to bring the shopping in

I see the pistol everywhere
    but it takes me weeks to realise
        that the one who brandishes the pistol
           is not the woman
but this man

Inventory

I drew up the inventory of my life:
at the age of fifty
after all that I have seen and done:
no property;
no savings;
two daughters, one of them 3500 miles away,
the other working out her issues with her therapist;
one extended family diaspora;
one about-to-be ex-wife;
two genuine friends;
one lover;
twenty unpublished books;
a million acquaintances and experiences;
one excellent job with moderate salary;
one reputation.

January 20th 2006

The man from the Israeli Government Tourist Office
wants to sell Israel to the children in my school
in the form of a gigantic Wonderland
from snow in the Hermon
all the way to the beaches of Eilat

The celluloid aeroplane spans the entire horizon
and if you're quick enough
or knowledgeable enough
you can point to all your favourite spots

Look there's Masada, Jerusalem, the Sea of Galilee
Aren't those children just having so much fun
surfing down the waterfalls at Banyas
floating on the surface of the Dead Sea
treading coral east of Aqaba

And all the date palms and the kibbutz kindergartens
the gum trees blooming in the Jezreel Valley
the bathing beauties on the beach in Tel Aviv
Why this could be Barbados
or the French Riviera

The man from the Israeli Government Tourist Office
thanks me for my time
thanks me for allowing him to make his presentation
at my school

When he leaves I check my e-mails
and find one from my cousin in Ramat Aviv
informing me somewhat despondently
that Hamas are now tipped to win next week's elections

Poem From A Random Line Of
Charles Bukowski[2]

Women were always beyond me
Between their figures and my eyes
a wall of fear induced procrastination
till the moment was inexorably lost

I could never tell if what I yearned for
in the act of giving and receiving
was what they also yearned for
in the act of giving and receiving

And though my brain told me it was
my soul retreated from the possibility of failure
my body shrivelled at the certainty of failure
and feint heart never won fair lady

So it is that I am standing here tonight
looking at the many splendid curves and cambers
in my own somewhat arch manner

Gazing into your eyes only
hoping maybe you will invite me
to tear down the wall

---

[2] The line in question is from "Young In New Orleans".

The Lace Of A Metaphor

Nietzsche never actually said that
"God is dead"
He simply found God dead
in the souls of His contemporaries

So when I sit here
pen in hand
and swell my soul with consciousness
of something tenuous
something unclear and incoherent
the lace of a metaphor
struggling to come through the mist

When I sit here
and God comes alive inside this poem
does that give me power over life and death
does that make me "mechayey meytim"
does that make me Messiah?

In the late summer of 2013, as I write this, I am enjoying a story
in the news media about a woman in Tennessee who named her
son Messiah, but was ordered by a magistrate to change it to Martin
on the grounds that only Jesus Christ could be given that name. A
higher court over-ruled this, not mentioning the fact that thousands
of young Hispanics are named Jesus, but on the grounds that the
judge had over-reached her authority, and there is a constitutional
separation between church and state. So Messiah is once again
Messiah, though he may be disappointed to learn that 354 other
boys in the United States have that name today, and none of them,
so far as has yet been demonstrated, have brought with them the
fulfilment of the kingdom.

The Marriage Of The Sacred And The Profane

O sing the marriage of divinity and love
the sanctification of the blessed prick and balls
the one John Donne sang to the holy dove
in the vestry of the Deanery at St Paul's

O sing the vows of Marian and Robin Hood
solemnised by venal Friar Tuck
and weave, as Durrell said we never should,
theology out of a mere fuck

Sing the "darling we have come through" song
that DHL sang up in Taos
unless of course the pubes prove to be wrong
in which case best go back to John Donne's louse

O sing the holy and the broken halleluyah
sing the wounding of the holy dove
sing the "love was truly pure before I knew yah"
sing the hand caressed by latex glove

Sing how man chase after woman till she catch him
sing the joy of both sides in the hunt
worship her as goddess made incarnate
baptise yourself within her holy font

Rejoice in the coniunctio spirituum
cross the tropics back and forth each night
recite the inner monologue of Molly Bloom
let Tristan meet Isolde when it's light

O sing the Whore of Babylon unsated
sing the trials of the Marquis de Sade
ask if Casanova was related
to that bawdy Newhouse mentioned by the bard

O sing of nymphomania and satyriasis
sing of marriage till death us do part
remember masturbation breeds psoriasis
while Kama Sutra transforms Love to Art

O sing the marriage of the sacred to profanity
let vice on earth be named virtue above
O sing in vain that blessed human vanity
the marriage of divinity and love

Of all the many poems that I elected to leave out of
this collection, the one I most wrestled with was a
poem entitled "For Agapé". Written in the late 1970s,
when I was a student, it was a response to a challenge
from a tutor, after a discussion about obscenity in
literature – Joyce's "Ulysses", Henry Miller's "Tropics",
Lawrence's "Lady Chatterley". Is it possible to tackle
the theme of profane love, using the profane words,
and still make poetry that is socially "acceptable" as
well as poetically valid? In 2008 that poem was used in
Toronto to justify an attack on me, and my school,
declaring me unfit to run a school if I wrote poems like
that. One part of me wants to include the poem, as an
act of defiance; but the truth is, this poem does it much
better, and "The Abalone Shell" likewise. "For Agapé"
is still on the Internet somewhere, if you really want to
read it.

A Poem Of Protest
Against The Protests
Against The Protests

This is the power of the Internet
global knowledge
universal intelligence

So I am able to learn that there are protests
over the cartoons of Mohammed
in London, Melbourne, across America;
that Kofi Annan has urged Moslems
to accept the apology from Denmark;
that editors have been fired in France and Jordan;
that some idiot of an American
First Ambassador for Religious Freedom
has noted that cartoons helped start the Holocaust;
that Palestinians have attacked the German consulate in Gaza
and Syrians torched the Norwegian Embassy in Damascus
mistaking it for the Danish;
that South Africans are alarmed that a court has banned
newspapers from publishing the cartoons
presumably, since this is the new South Africa,
equally in black and white or colour;
that an Imam in Sacramento has called on Moslems
to "respond with measured protest";
while the President of Pakistan has called for "jihad"
and 4,000 marchers in Morocco have sworn to make of this
the catalyst for the overthrow of Zionism
and the satanic empire of the United States.

This is the power of the power of the Internet
global knowledge
universal intelligence
allowing me to witness moment by moment
the power of the power of hysteria:
global stupidity
universal ignorance

These Are The Significant Moments

Phoning my parents
  to tell them I am getting a divorce
  and realising I had to tell my mother
  not my father

Deciding which friends need to be informed
  and how precisely to phrase it in my e-mail

Hearing back immediately
  from one such friend
  within minutes by e-mail
  within the hour by telephone;

Driving through icy winds
  and rain
  and treacherous snow
so my new woman
  can show me where she grew up
  and make love with me
  in her bedroom at her parents' flat

Waking up the next morning
  to hear my father on the telephone
  needing to have his own turn
  at my mother's conversation

Moments of recognition
  of endorsement
  of confirmation

Two Poems For LC

1. To My Zen-Master

I read Ira Nadel's biography of you
and it became clear that poetry
has never been your purpose
but only your device
an expediency in the greater goal
which is seduction:

to find a form of words
a tone of voice
a rhythm or a cadence or construction
a schmooze in short
whether speaking casually
reciting verse
or singing songs

to find the means of getting one young woman
or one entire audience
to let you fall in love
with yourself

Once upon a time there was a young poet and
novelist named Leonard Cohen, who turned to
writing songs and singing his poems, and became
an object of scorn, derision and satire in intellectual
circles. "Music to commit suicide by" was one
verdict. "Songs for lonely bedsit girls" was another.
And as to his novel, "Beautiful Losers", it was
condemned as the consequences of an LSD trip and
the self-indulgence of a religious sex-maniac. To like
LC was to invite mockery; to learn to sing and play
every one of his songs was simply contemptible. I
learned to sing and play every one of his songs.
Today, half a century later, he stands in the Hall of
Fame as one of the greatest of his generation. Was
it not ever thus!

2. The Plagiarist

For you
I will be a penitent Lothario
offer you a fair dowry
an unambitious stepmother
and name you my Calista
in exchange for being named your Lovelace

For you
I will be a contrite Casanova
compare love to an incurable illness
and a divine monster
give you proofs that God is still alive
and magic still afoot

For you
I will be a mortified Don Juan
sail from Cadiz until I'm shipwrecked
then live in the seraglio
disguised as a female slave
and conquer Ismail in your name

For you
I will stand in the window of the Bastille
while they guillotine John Thomas and Queen Jane
then throw away the whips and rancid butter
vow to speak only of true love in the early dawn
and mean each word of it

For you
I will be the poet laureate of Canada
sing lyric poems to an out of tune guitar
from a stage beneath your balcony
and recount the entire history of lust
over and over
until you fall for me

To S, By E-Mail

Whatever happened to the love letters
that we used to write
the daily dance of courtship
on a parquet floor in cyberspace?

Does love grow so familiar
it becomes a habit
something that one simply does
like shopping for the groceries?

And if it is
then please
next time you're in the store

one pack of reinstated romance
two litres of kisses
a box of hugs

some of that paper towel you like to use
to wipe away the errors flaws and weaknesses
and make the table neat and clean again

and if they have any
because it's a very rare commodity
a jar or two of Quality Time
frankly any size will do

Today The Sea Is Beautiful

Today the sea is beautiful
shimmering white beyond the city
an illusion of ice in the sunny morning

I sit by the window
updating my webpage

eating herring and Boursin
on fresh warm Viennese bread

drinking Wissotzky tea
brought back to me from Israel
as a gift

far from the rigours of the day-job
or the demands of the outer life

calm as lake-birds
placid as chimney-smoke
serene as the psalms I would be singing
if I had gone to shul this shobbas morning

writing the beauty of the sea
the shimmering whiteness of regeneration
the illusion of peace on this sunny morning

The Ballad Of The Sick Child

'Twas Wednesday noon, at half past twelve
The migraine clouds were rising
The sky was blue as frozen hands
And dark was the horizon

"Come down, come down" the VP called,
"Your daughter's gone and feinted
We need your consent on the form
The ambulance is waiting

Her friends have brought her to the nurse
Her knees were almost crumbling
Her fever's high and getting worse
She cannot walk for stumbling"

By half past one on Gerrard Street
The stretcher bearers parted
The vitals read, the forms complete
The data neatly charted

An ECG, her heart is fine
The blood work reveals little
Her eyes have got some hazy shine
There's sodium in her spittle

This neckache though is worrisome -
Meningus or the cushion?
Tap the knees and squeeze the flesh
Push here and keep on pushing

There's nothing wrong, there's nothing wrong
They've tested her to zero
Idiopathic prognoses
Best treated with placebo

But first an anti-migraine drug
Use IV for the saline
Then send her father out to buy
Some cheap chlorpromazine

From pharmacist to pharmacist
Like Bruce in Patagonia
Hunting for millennial cures
For an inflamed hypochondria

By half past nine the pills were home
And she already dozing
The migraine clouds were lifted now
The blue, turned black, still frozen

*

'Twas Thursday noon, round half past twelve
The feinting spell was spoken
Abracadabra down she fell
Belief in cures was broken

Again the blue-lamp chariot
Again they came to fetch her
Wrapped in blankets, cuddling bear
Downtown on a stretcher

Again the tests, again the drip
Look out for signs and warnings
In fear the patient patient waits
For night to turn to morning

But CT scan showed negative
And ECG was normal
Precautionary appointments made
The discharge notice formal

'Twas Friday noon, at half past twelve
The migraine clouds were rising
The sky was blue as frozen hands
But lighter the horizon

Two Lovers

Two lovers meet, but do not touch.
What was it like? each asks.
She was beautiful, he says, but rather passive;
timid with her mouth and casual with her hands;
but lovely flesh, and o so loud at orgasm
the neighbours started banging on the walls.
And what of him?
O, he was handsome, very cocksure,
though in truth he had little to be cocksure about;
greedy for his own gratification,
wanting to touch for his own pleasure, not for mine;
and timid too, like yours,
when I suggested certain sensualities.
Will you see him again, he asks?
Tonight, he's asked me out for dinner
and we're staying at a hotel.
What about you, will you see her again?
I don't suppose so.
She was coy enough about this one occasion.
But if you're staying at a hotel, how will we meet,
when will we make love?
Tomorrow, she says,
and I promise to tell you every detail.
So the lovers touch, and part,
each bound by their total fidelity, one to the other,
each conscious that the lover they had spoken of
had gone home racked by guilt at infidelity.

Union Negotiation

Given that we are colleagues
and in many cases friends
the entire process is ridiculous
us at one end of the table
them down at the other
speaking through lawyers
the way that God and Man
are incapable of dialogue
unless through priests

We are not permitted so much
as the movement of a facial muscle
a wriggling let alone a squirming
in our seats

no interventions
no whisperings
nothing that gives our game away
only if needs be a call to caucus

This process
which is called negotiation
and is intended to obtain
collective agreement
defines us as adversaries
puts up barriers and barricades
and will eventually collapse
in strife and enmity

- unless at some point I intervene
and do again
what I did to simplify the process last year:
sack the lawyer

Vergangenheitsbewältung[3]

I began to learn German
when I was very young

I learned
first
that the German language
is a compound language
where words are joined with words
to make new words

as past events are joined
with past events
to make new nations

I learned
for example
Vergangenheitsbewältung

A truly beautiful expression
of the modern German language
which I took much pleasure learning

only to discover
it was virtually unknown
in Germany

---

[3] The process of coming to terms with the past.

Write This In Black

I spend long hours surveying the inner darkness
hoping to find new ways of naming it
hoping of course for art love music poetry or God
But inner worlds are only mirror images of outer worlds
where art graffitoes love rapes music screams
and poetry and God grow indistinguishable
love-flesh flesh-love

Hence the quantity of blackened pages
hence the writing of these words in black

Yet even black does not smudge the whiteness underneath
even darkness can break open with a crack

Continue In Grey

Continue in grey
Which is what happens
When black and white conjoin
Like human bodies in the act of love
The brutality of beauty

When I Was Young

When I was young I interviewed myself incessantly,
needing to know the sources of what seemed a spark;
the answers came out, flickering fluorescently,
not yet illumination though no longer dark.

Who am I? was the general gist of the interrogation,
with touches of where from? and hints of why? and how?
and even, though I had as yet no sense of destination,
an asking, an imploring, for a unity of when? and now.

The interview, the dialogue, remained internal,
a speaking to myself albeit in a stranger's tones,
but speaking till I chewed the nut down to the kernel
and ground the meat to gristle and revealed the bones.

The dialogue, the interview, the conversation -
whatever you prefer to name this act of thought –
led to some most surprising intellectual revelations,
even at times to insights that were really rather neatly wrought,

led – this is what I want to tell you – to an understanding
far deeper than I could have gleaned from books or friends,
far deeper than I could have gleaned from someone handing
me the data they'd acquired through their own convex lens.

The interviews themselves were all contemptibly hubristic,
some Radio 4 arts programme, some press conference post-Nobel,
a discussion with a monarch, or a maestro, or a mystic,
some disciple from the future saying what had made me such a swell

But the purpose wasn't vanity or ego-swelling arrogance;
my narcissism was intended only to explain,
and only to myself, and hopefully with eloquence,
those existential questions that one yearns to ascertain.

Now forty years have passed me by and still the light is flickering,
and absolute uncertainty is all that I've achieved,
and still the voices in my head are arguing and bickering,
whether darkness can be lifted, whether light can be perceived.

And the monarch has departed, and the maestro has retired,
and the mystic made a vow to let the silence apprehend;
someone else received the Nobel and my radio expired,
but my interviews continue, and will do so till the end.

For a Catholic there are priest-boxes in which to make confession.
For atheists a couch whereon the mind can dig and delve.
But me I much prefer this strange, eccentrical obsession,
this likely madness too, I guess, of talking to myself.

A Jew Finds Comfort And Familiarity
At A Christian Funeral

At Monica's mother's funeral
a 7th Day Adventist chapel down in Mississauga
a most un-Christian place it seemed
a building like a warehouse
a shrine with no icons
a chapel with no rest
(the vigour of the oratory
and the energy of the responses
neither permitted nor tolerated rest)
a place of light despite
the lack of stained-glass windows

And o Lord what vigour in that oratory
yay Jesus what energy in those responses
the vehemence of faith in every speech (yes, brother)
the ardour of belief in every utterance (amen)
the fervour of conviction behind every cry (sing, sister)
the passion of devotion behind every hymn (yay, Lord)

A very un-Christian place indeed
despite the quotes from Timothy and Thessalonians
everything else was Psalms and Prophets
long excerpts from Ecclesiastes
poured out like honeyed rap
by a Jamaican bishop
with his eyes closed
and the text engraved in memory
like the Ten Commandments on their slabs of stone

No need for icons
Scripture itself has become the icon
The Holy of Holies is the human heart and mind
empty except to those empowered to see
what is only visible through the lens of prophecy

In this world no one ever dies

Simply a soul travels
from the world's waiting room
on the train of death
down the stations of the Cross
to the terminus of Heaven
and we look forward to the day
(yes, brother)
when we will greet our friends and neighbours there
(amen)

Simply we are loaned life
the way a pawnbroker is lent some precious object
and when the moment is opportune
it is redeemed

The Laws Of Nature

When we speak about the "Laws of Nature"
it is important to understand
that we do not mean laws
in the judicial sense
of rules and regulations
for breach of which
a heretical flower
or an apostate tree
may be punished
by burning in an auto-da-fé
a blasphemous fish deported from its native waters
a recalcitrant swallow ousted from its nest
and hung
by its splayed digits
or worse
its neck
or nailed sado-masochistically
like a human on a Cross

When we speak about the "Laws of Nature"
we mean only
those identifiable if inconstant patterns
of general behaviour
which seem
with considerable flexibility
much variation
and sufficient exceptions
to furnish complete proof

and not proof of the homogeneity of Nature
not proof that all creatures must obey or die
not proof that anything is certain or predictable
not proof that good is good and bad is bad
not proof of ugliness or beauty
not proof of planned or happenstance
but simply proof by logic
that there is no earthly need
or use
for God

The New Order

I read in the Talmud
that if a man has boils
or bad body odour
he is obliged to divorce his wife

This is how it should be
This is how we shall build
the new world order

Men who fail to clean their minds properly
will lose their human status

Men who cook with too much ginger
will be compelled to sleep with insects

Men who walk on the grass
will be made to smoke it

Men who write foolish laws
will be compelled to keep them

This is the rule of the new world order

Obey

or be disbarred from eternity

THE WORD AND THE TEMPLE
(2013)

辞　Pronounced, I believe, Shi, the Chinese character for poetry incorporates the ideograms of both "the word" and "the temple", which makes a wonderful parallel, in contrast, with the caged songbird of the muses; the concept of shrine is there intrinsically, the sacredness of the act of reflection that leads to the act of writing, as well as the words themselves, once reflection is made flesh.

In reality there is no collection by this name; as the date should give away. After the completion of "Tortoise", I have not published again, waiting for this book, knowing I would include any new poems here. But the title is irresistible, and the excuse for a Chinese ideogram even more so.

From A Stretched Limo

It is not my usual custom to write verses
To a woman I am smitten with by love
God spare me sentiment that just rehearses
The chivalry of kissing on the glove

God spare me saccharine gestures made of verbiage
And platitudes passed off as profound wit
And imitation Romeos by Burbage
And sententious "Love Is" this or that bullshit

It is not my usual custom to write verses
To a woman I am smitten with by love
Most likely all I'll get back is her curses
Or slapped for trying my chivalry on her glove

So unless you're an Italian or Frenchman
Whose language offers love means to propose
Much better send your lady, through some henchman,
A copy of Dot Parker's "Perfect Rose"

Or even better take advice from Dotty
Remember that it's celluloid not silver screen
Forget the verses they'll just drive you potty
And leave the roses in the limousine.

A Foot

A foot is not a foot without a limp
A face is not a face without a scar
Love is never love without a quarrel
But daytime is still daytime without stars

A Journey Into Rhyme

I set out on a journey into rhyme
to see what freedom may be found there
It does not take a great amount of time
to understand I am already bound there

The lines upon the page rule my direction
The margins set the limit of my scope
But infinite capacities of diction
defy the inclination to lose hope

A single word suffices to deliver
freedom to the dungeon or the cell
From Devil's Island swim away down-river
to where the butterflies enlighten Hell

Then chain me like Prometheus' eagle
compelled to watch the liver outlive pain
Fetter me in garb stately and regal
constrained to clothe the emperor again

Open up the boundaries and borders
Unlock the wrought iron prison gate
Issue me a free man's marching orders
Let gaol itself empower me to create

And give me words like God in the beginning
imbued with absolute creative might
Atlases of Ariadne's spinning
Labyrinths of waxen, wingèd light

Bury me in lexicons of leather
Weigh me down with coffin-loads of texts
Lear my soul through heaths of stormy weather
Guide me through the guide for the perplexed

Virgil me on journeys beyond never
dictionaries my dreams misunderstood
Grant me strength to raise my sword and sever
the knots that fetter the enchanted wood

Sancho me on journeys beyond rhyming
Show me what exists beyond the found
Grant me more of tempo less of timing
and let me know at last I am unbound

Haiku Of 21 Syllables

Lady you are beautiful
said I
But her look of disbelief
was truly ugly

An Arborealist Faces Up To Reality

this poem ought to have been carved
on the bark of a tree
but was in fact scratched on parchment paper
made by running sheets of paper pulp
through baths of sulphuric acid

Shakespeare picked the red, red rose
but I worry about leaf-curl

Pound chose lily of the valley
but I found fungus

Hilton built paradise in Shangri-La
but concrete gets cankerous

Buddha sat under the Bodhi tree
A Dutch Elm, sadly.

So many diseases
affecting so many plants:

Wheels that come off the Cyclamen
Fire that turns whole forests into Ash
Hummingbirds that peck the eyes of Black-Eyed Susan
Anti-biotics that fail with Feverfew and Feverbush
Trampling feet which reduce the Goldenglow
Fronds that strangle the Lovevine
Viruses that wound the Bleeding Heart

Forget global warming
The real threat to the survival of the planet
Is Nature itself

For Wallace Stevens

Too tired to create
I went hunting for inspiration
at the Academy of American Poets
and after rejecting a dozen
perfectly decent scribblers
simply because their tone
did not match my inner needs
at that precise moment
I came upon Wallace Stevens
and stayed till it was night

Coming back again a few days later
I discovered
that Stevens only began publishing in his fifties
a walking tour of Hartford fit for Leo Bloom
the belief that poetry is the supreme fiction
an alleged death-bed conversion to Catholicism
the poem of the mind
in the act of finding
          what will suffice
a career in insurance
just like Einstein and Kafka
a candle
burning alone in an immense valley
until the wind blew
until the wind blew

In Defence Of Günter Grass

Who is the greater German:
Grass or Hermann Hesse?
Hermann joined the pacifists
Grass the Waffen SS

They want to take his Nobel Prize
and shove it up his arse
Politics trumps literature
in the case of Günter Grass

They want to take his Nobel Prize
and stuff it down his throat
You fools - this misses the whole point
Honour what he wrote

How should dishonoured Germany
face up to its guilt?
It seems this was his motive
in every word he spilt

Yes, spilt. The blood of Germany
bleeds through his every line
If he was a fool at seventeen
These books have paid his fine

And what about the Peace prizes
To Kissinger and Arafat?
I say you should revoke those too
but there's no chance of that

This outrage against Günter
resounds like a hollow hum
drowned out by majestic beating
from an unrustable tin drum

Marriage

Getting married
is not the same as
being married

The one an opportunity
to be a royal
for a day

The other
fifty years of sovereignty

The one
the swearing of a vow

The other
the fulfilling of it

Divorce is merely
the recognition
of a lapsed covenant
and a tarnished crown

Poem Of Failure

I tried to pray, but the silence was ineffable
I tried to sleep, but the ghosts of daytime infiltrated
I tried to write, but the page rebelled against me
I tried to read, but thought diverted me
I tried to walk...

  no, this is not the way

I tried to pray, but the silence was ineffable
I tried to stifle silence, but the gag was chewed and torn
I tried to mend the gag, but it mocked me viciously
I tried an experiment in vice, but did so virtuously...

  better, but still not right

I tried to pray, but failed
I tried to sleep, but failed
I tried to write, and wrote these lines
  which failed

Sometimes
  like tonight
        the act of failure
                is itself the poem
                        achieved
out of the act of struggle

Prose-Poem For An Unnamed Woman

What must it be like to be desired by every man who ever sees you every man who walks past you in the street who stands next to you at the check-out in the supermarket who sits opposite you in a restaurant who slows down your progress in a line who deliberately rubs up against you in a crowded train who passes by your house and cannot resist a glimpse through the uncurtained window and not even voyeuristically in the hope of seeing you naked but simply in the hope of seeing you at all of having the sun shine on him more potently as a consequence of seeing you not even imagining making love to you just knowing you are there that the place you occupy on Earth will always be a place of beauty simply because the angle of your jaw the shape of your hips a series of geometric accidents a metabolism over which you have zero control a chance genetic inheritance a fashion in faces and figures the woman next to you is actually a finer human being the ugly woman the fat one with the glasses and the hare-lip more generous more intellectual less egotistical the truth is from personal as well as anecdotal evidence you are actually a bitch of the first order a narcissistic monomaniacal bitch who treats her husband terribly and her children even worse who eats lovers for breakfast who any man with any sense should scrupulously avoid but still your face your form your smile the blueness of your eyes the blondeness of your hair to stand in your presence is to receive the glow of radiance that pours from you to be invested with a privilege to be joined in harmony with all mankind in certainty that all share this same honour this same adoration which you in fact despise

Song Of Absence

Do not come home for me.
Come because your presence here is necessary.
The cats need you.
The kids need you.
The mirror in the bathroom needs you.
The Camembert is turning sour.
The tofu is growing something inorganic.
The lady at the check-out keeps asking after you.
Your therapist is anxious to schedule an appointment.
Do not come home for me.
Come because your presence here is necessary.

The Hero

Dragged to the gallows
kicking and screaming
while the TV editors wondered
whether to keep filming
or to cut to shots of the crowd
the President
the traitor's tearful family
they finally got him tied and bound

The executioner took off his gag
to allow him the traditional last word
"Damn the god-damned bloody lot of you!"
he screamed
though not quite so politely as recorded here
but a technical hitch cut off the sound
and anyway it was time
        for a commercial break.

Two Sets Of Thoughts
While Driving Home Along Jarvis Street

1.

First snow.
You can tell how cold it is
by the fact that
even the whores
have flown indoors
for the winter.

2.

It is quite erroneous
to say a prostitute
is a woman who sells her body

To sell is to relinquish
to the purchaser
for all time

To sell is to transfer ownership

Prostitutes rent out their bodies
in specific blocks of time
then take them back

It is in traditional marriage
that women sell their bodies

Song Of Nothing

We had
    we realised
        absolutely nothing

(which is of course
    still a kind of possession
        and therefore something)

nothing that is
    except one thing:
        the money with which to purchase nothing

So we devoted our lives
    to the acquisition of money

and this we achieved by
    producing and selling
        as much nothing as possible

It was still nothing of course
    but it had become
a different kind of something
    a valuable nothing
and some of it had designer labels
and some of it was advocated by the famous
and some of it had been discarded by the infamous
and some of it glistered and glowed like gold
and some of it was tacky and kitschy
but what an abundance of nothing it surely was
and what an amazing nation we must be
the richest in nothing in the history of the world
transmuters of dross into gold
    of nothing into something
        which is still nothing
    it's true
but what extraordinarily
    valuable
        nothing

A something in its own right

It was only when I was collating these poems for this collection that I realised I had already written "Song For Nothing", in the poem entitled "Beauty". But then again, perhaps they are not quite the same poem. The English teacher in me would love to sit down with a group of students and invite them to parse both, to extrapolate the differences as well as the similarities, and especially to debate the ideas that underlie the two. Sadly there is little left of readership of poetry but such students, and most of them, through bad teaching, regard the exercise as little different from dissecting frogs in the laboratory; or maybe even worse, because at least frogs are yuck.

The Artist At Work

A need –
a truly primitive need –
within the soul
the heart
the mind
the body
simply to make marks
on otherwise blank canvas:
paper or cave wall

A second
  parallel
        complementary need
the need of a sophisticated life-form
to utilise the available mental energy
and fill the space that would otherwise be
  boredom

Becomes a doodle
  incoherent and unarticulated
        devoid of lucidity

Becomes a mathematical pattern
  gradually acquiring logic
        symmetry

Becomes totemic
  abstract art

Becomes figurative

Or else becomes letters
  scribbled
        printed
                calligraphed

built into words
   phrases
       sentences
          books

Either way it takes the primal need
   conjoins it with the sophisticated need
      and makes of it a form
of human self-expression

The Ascetic

Every day
10,000 eyes follow you through the streets,
each one kindled by the same desire,
each one yearning to hold you in exactly the same way,
to touch you, kiss you, in exactly the same places,
to repeat with you the singular, identical possibility,
that curiously narrow range of options
available to a man and woman,
repeated by 1,000,000,000 couples
every day;
to seek in them some sacred magic
that will render this act of coupling unique,
until they are reduced to the same disappointment,
not simply the recognition that it is all singular, identical,
but the impossibility of recovering the one thing
that did make this encounter different, special, sacred,
the impossibility of recovering
what I have and hold and am sworn never to lose,
which is the kindling moment of desire.

The End Of Books

The reason there will never be an end of books is not
As you might think
From love of books

The book is merely a form
But what it contains
Is magical and irreplaceable
And just as coins need purses
And treasures need chests
So words need books
To stop them spilling out
Or being lost or stolen

We who read but do not write
Or write
But only middling indifferently
We live our lives so inarticulately
And revere those who make order
From the hazard and the chaos

The end of books will come
Only with the end of magic

That is to say
When we cease to dream
To yearn
To imagine
The perfections that exist beyond our grasp

Yedid Nephesh meets Lecha Dodi

This poem was written as a challenge at a conference of Jewish educators. We were given fifteen minutes to make something creative out of the lines of the two great Friday evening hymns. This was our offering.

Please my beloved it's time to decide
    I'll be your soulmate if you'll be my guide
Hasten love, show love, together abide
    I'll be your David if you'll be my bride
Show me your grace, let love never hide
    I'll be your soulmate if you'll be my guide
In your shelter of peace let our two souls abide
    I'll be your David if you'll be my bride
Show me your mercy, let your arms open wide
    I'll be your soulmate if you'll be my guide
Strengthen me, heal me, let no tears be cried
    I'll be your David if you'll be my bride
Let your sweet love delight me, let it not be denied
    I'll be your soulmate if you'll be my guide
That we may rejoice and be glad without pride
    I'll be your David if you'll be my bride

Zero Positive

If I could be anything in this world
I would like to be a zero

You, I know, would rather be a one
And find some other one
To be a two with

Or maybe several other ones
And become three, four, five

But me, I would like to be a zero
Of no value on my own
But put me with any other one
And our value is increased
Tenfold

Zhana

Zhana the snow-queen
from Nizhny-Novgorod
tall and blonde as a snowdrop
in a fun-fur made of icicles

I seem to be drawn
to Russian women
the tall slim ones especially
like fir trees in the tundra

I showed her my photographs
from Nizhny-Novgorod
the Soviet headquarters
and the Duma

the red fort with its military museum
cars buried under six feet of snow
old folks at the Jewish
community centre by the synagogue

and when she left
I resumed my re-reading of
Going To The Wall
and heated up a bowl of borscht

Then maybe that elusive template of female beauty, the model of
desire, wasn't K at all. Maybe it was Z for Zhana.

A Song Of Gratitude

Thank you, good friends, thank you
I'm honoured to be here
Offering my thank yous
as a boost to my career

I'd like to start by thanking
my agent and my wife
but alas my agent sacked me
and my wife – I mean my ex-wife...

I'd like to thank my lucky stars
(I'm not the sort for whining)
That my silver cloud is silver-lined
(Though there's damage to the lining)

I'd like to thank my mum and dad
For the way that I've been risen
My mother for her English skills
(my dad is still in prison)

I'd like to thank my countrymen
for making me a patriot
and teaching me that love is always
relative to hatred

I'd like to thank my affluence
for arriving uninvited
but could I ask one favour more –
my lust's still unrequited

I'd like to thank the gods for promising
the harmony of nations
and peace for all mankind and specially
endowing us with patience

I'd like to thank the management
the caterers and technicians
for making things seem squeaky-clean
like perfect politicians

I'd like to thank Columbus
for discovering the Bahamas
and Mahler for his symphonies
and Shakespeare for his dramas

I'd like to thank each one of you
for making a donation
Please write "D Prashker" on the cheque -
then "Charitable Foundation"

I'd like to thank the lady
in the third row, seat 4C
for generously offering
to come home tonight with me

I'd like to thank the hand of fate
for the portion I've been given
May all its fingers be cut off
its guilty soul be shriven

I'd like to thank the Royal Family
and work hard to preserve it
I'd like to thank them – honestly –
but the buggers don't deserve it

I'd like to thank each one of you
for coming to this poem
I'd raise a glass or two with you
but I quaffed the jeroboam

And finally thank you to those folk
who invented thank you speeches
May your spirits live eternally
deep in the nether reaches

Thank you and good night

Poems do not normally offer alternative lines and verses, though I really can't see why they shouldn't, and many poems come to mind that would clearly benefit. However, on this occasion, because this poem is itself an ending – the ending of the book - I would just like to say a very big thank you to the proof-reader who returned her copy with this suggestion for a better closing line for the opening stanza.

Thank you, good friends, thank you
I'm honoured to be here
Offering my thank yous
however insincere

I'd also like to thank my editor, my publisher, my spiritual counsellor, my lawyer, my therapist, my accountant and of course my mistress, just for being there guys, just for being there.

ABOUT THE AUTHOR

 David Prashker
was born in London in 1955 and has lived
in France, Israel, Canada and the United
States, where he is currently based.

He is the author of thirty books, including
contemporary and historical novels, short
stories, poetry, songs, plays and scholarly
works. You can follow his blog at
apps.theargamanpress.com/Blog/ or find
him at his website Davidprashker.com.

For more information about his books, go
to:
theargamanpress.com.

www.ingramcontent.com/pod-product-compliance
Lightning Source LLC
LaVergne TN
LVHW051047080426
835508LV00019B/1757